DWIGHT GARNER

Garner's Quotations

Dwight Garner is a book critic for *The New York Times* and was previously the senior editor of *The New York Times Book Review*. His essays and criticism have also appeared in *The New Republic*, *Harper's Magazine*, *Slate*, and other publications.

ALSO BY DWIGHT GARNER

Read Me: A Century of Classic American Book Advertisements

Garner's Quotations

Garner's Quotations

{ A MODERN MISCELLANY }

Dwight Garner

PICADOR FARRAR, STRAUS AND GIROUX {New York}

Picador

120 Broadway, New York 10271

Printed in the United States of America

Originally published in 2020 by Farrar, Straus and Giroux

First paperback edition, 2021

Owing to limitations of space, all acknowledgments for permission to reprint previously published material can be found on pages 287–288.

The Library of Congress has cataloged the Farrar, Straus and Giroux hardcover edition as follows:

Names: Garner, Dwight, author.

Title: Garner's quotations : a modern miscellany / Dwight Garner.

Description: First edition. | New York : Farrar, Straus and Giroux, 2020. | Includes index.

Identifiers: LCCN 2020026942 | ISBN 9780374279196 (hardcover)

Subjects: LCSH: Commonplace books. | Quotations, English.

Classification: LCC PN6245 .G37 2020 | DDC 081—dc23

LC record available at https://lccn.loc.gov/2020026942

Paperback ISBN: 978-1-250-80022-0

Designed by Richard Oriolo

Our books may be purchased in bulk for promotional, educational, or business use. Please contact your local bookseller or the Macmillan Corporate and Premium Sales Department at 1-800-221-7945, extension 5442, or by email at MacmillanSpecialMarkets@macmillan.com.

For book club information, please visit facebook.com/picadorbookclub or email marketing@picadorusa.com.

picadorusa.com • instagram.com/picador

twitter.com/picadorusa • facebook.com/picadorusa

10   9   8   7   6   5   4   3   2   1

For Cree

Sometimes it seems the only accomplishment my education ever bestowed on me, the ability to think in quotations.
—MARGARET DRABBLE, *A SUMMER BIRD-CAGE*

The primary object of a student of literature is to be delighted.
—LORD DAVID CECIL

PREFACE

> { Make your own Bible. Select and collect all
> those words and sentences that in all your
> reading have been to you like the blast of a
> trumpet out of Shakespeare, Seneca, Moses,
> John, and Paul. } —RALPH WALDO EMERSON

For nearly four decades, I've kept what's known as a commonplace book. It's where I write down favorite sentences from novels, stories, poems, and songs, from plays and movies, from overheard conversations. Lines that made me sit up in my seat; lines that jolted me awake. About once a year, I'll say something I think is worthy of inclusion. I mostly end up deleting those entries.

{ I began keeping my commonplace book in the 1980s, when I was in high school. In the 1990s, when I was working as the arts editor for an alternative weekly newspaper in Vermont, I typed the whole thing into a long computer file. I've moved it from desktops to laptops and now onto my iPhone, too. Into it I've poured verbal delicacies, "the blast of a trumpet," as Emerson put it, and bits of scavenged wisdom from my life as a reader. Yea, for I am an underliner, a destroyer of books, and maybe you are, too.

{ Commonplace books are not so uncommon. Virginia Woolf kept one. So did Samuel Johnson. W. H. Auden published his, as did the poet J. D. McClatchy. E. M. Forster's was issued after his death. The novelist David Markson wrote terse and enveloping novels that resembled commonplace books; they were bird's nests of facts threaded with the author's own subtle interjections. For fans of the genre, many prize examples have come from lesser-known figures such as Geoffrey Madan and Samuel Rogers, both English, who issued commonplace books that are notably generous and witty and illuminating. These have become cult items. The literary critic Christopher Ricks said about Rogers that, although he may not have been a kind man, "he was very good at hearing what was said."

{ In my commonplace book, for handy reference, I keep things in categories: "food," "conversation," "social class," "travel," "politics," "cleanliness," "war," "money," "clothing," etc. I use it as an aide-mémoire, a kind of external hard drive. It helps me ward off what Christopher

Hitchens, quoting a friend, called CRAFT (Can't Remember a Fucking Thing) syndrome. I use my gleanings in my own writing. Like Montaigne, I quote others "in order to better express myself." Montaigne compared quoting well to arranging other people's flowers. Sometimes, I sense, I quote too often in the reviews I write for *The New York Times*, swinging on quotations as if from vine to vine. It's one of the curses of spending a lifetime as a word-eater, and of retaining a reliable memory. Perhaps the book you are holding will purge me of this habit. I fear it will inflame it.

{ I am no special fan of most books of quotations. *Bartlett's Familiar Quotations*, *The Yale Book of Quotations*, and *The New Penguin Dictionary of Modern Quotations*, to name three dependable reference books, are invaluable, for sure, as repositories of literary and verbal history. (Countless other books of quotations aren't reliable at all, and the less said about quotation sites on the Internet the better.) But even the best contain a good deal of dead weight. They lean, sometimes necessarily, on canned and overused thought and, grievously, are skewed to the upbeat. So many of the lines they contain seem to vie to be stitched onto throw pillows or ladled, like soup, over the credulous soul. "Almost all poetry is a failure," Charles Bukowski contended, "because it sounds like somebody saying, Look, I have written a poem." The same is true of quotations and aphorisms. So many have a taxidermied air, as if they were self-consciously aimed at posterity.

{ The book you are holding is a more personal venture. It's an attempt to break with the conventions of commonplace books and volumes of quotations. For one thing, it contains only a small selection of the material I've hoarded. For another, in arranging these sentences I've gone by feel, not by category. I've tried to let the comments speak to one another and perhaps throw off unexpected sparks.

{ Quotations, by definition, are out of context. I've played freely with this notion and have placed some lines quite out of context indeed. In this book there are few life lessons and little uplift, except by accident. I've selected lines mostly from books and writers I admire, and it's my hope that a reading list might present itself over the course of the proceedings. This book is a way of saying thank you to many writers for the pleasure they've brought me. Obviously I don't agree with everything said; retweet does not always, as they say on Twitter, equal endorsement.

{ A literary critic thinks long and hard before bringing another book into the world. Perhaps, this critic thinks, a thrifty book that points the way to other books might be worthwhile. Walt Whitman, in an article published posthumously in *The Atlantic*, declared that he was tired of "gloved gentleman words." He admired "unhemmed latitude, coarseness, directness, live epithets, expletives, words of opprobrium, resistance." I have tried to put Whitman's words to use in regard to quotations. There is more blaspheming in this book than there is in most collections of quotations. (Until fairly recently, most did not permit profanity.) It is a truth universally acknowledged among book critics that the most memorable lines in many novels contain the word *fuck*. These cannot be printed in newspapers. I have saved these lines up, and present some of them here.

—Dwight Garner

Garner's Quotations

I hope this pen works. Yes, it does.
> —Katherine Mansfield, diary

How're you doing, apart from the end of liberal capitalist democracy?
> —Ali Smith, *Spring*

A friend of mine says this is the beginning of the end of the global order.
> —Rachel Cusk, *Coventry*

One day someone will use the last surviving Latin word in English to say something like, This sucks.
> —Michael Hofmann, *Paris Review* interview

I've heard the saying "That sucks" for years without really being sure of what it meant. Now I think I know.
> —Stephen King, *The Stand*

I wonder what the *nice* people are doing tonight.
> —Chelsey Minnis, "Iceberg"

Why are you all reading? I don't understand this reading business when there is so much fucking to be done.
> —Sheila Heti, *How Should a Person Be?*

Better a good venereal disease than a moribund peace and quiet.

> —Henry Miller, *Quiet Days in Clichy*

—They've got crabs.
—What's wrong with that? I asked. We eat crabs all the time.

> —Henry Louis Gates, Jr., *Colored People*

Here we go then, (genital) warts an' all . . .

> —Viv Albertine, *Clothes, Clothes, Clothes. Music, Music, Music.*
> *Boys, Boys, Boys.*

Everything that is true is inappropriate.

> —Oscar Wilde

Everyone nodded, nobody agreed.

> —Ian McEwan, *Amsterdam*

Let's, as if sore, grab a few things from the flood.

> —A. R. Ammons, "Sphere: The Form of a Motion"

Fragments, indeed. As if there were anything to break.

> —Don Paterson, *Best Thought, Worst Thought*

—He licked his lips. Well, if you want my opinion—
—I don't, she said. I have my own.

> —Toni Morrison, *Beloved*

Love poems must be bounced back off a moon.

> —Robert Graves, *Paris Review* interview

See the moon? It hates us.

> —Donald Barthelme, *Sixty Stories*

The moon, big as a Bitcoin.

> —Jeanette Winterson, *Frankissstein*

Supposing one fell onto the moon.

> —D. H. Lawrence, "Indians and an Englishman"

Moon's left town. Moon's clean gone.

> —James Michie, "Arizona Nature Myth"

You know where the Beatles got that shit from. You know that's our shit they fucking up like that.

> —Albert Murray, *South to a Very Old Place*

How come the Beatles never got busted for statutory rape—because they're white?

> —Eve Babitz, *Eve's Hollywood*

I hope you don't mind, I'm from the South, we're touchers.

> —Charlie Rose, attributed

Mick Jagger should fold up his penis and go home.

> —Robert Christgau, in *The Village Voice*

—How's everything with you?

—Absolutely marvelous!

—Shit.

> —Bernard Malamud and Brendan Gill, in conversation

Somehow he knew, based on very little experience, that this *faux*-casual shit spelled *money*.

> —Tom Wolfe, *The Bonfire of the Vanities*

If you want to know what God thinks of money, just look at the people he gave it to.

> —Dorothy Parker, attributed

Tweedy shitballs.

> —Calvin Trillin's term for boarding-school types, *Remembering Denny*

I'll have no college swankies.

> —James Joyce, *Finnegans Wake*

Oh, fuck, not another elf!

> —Hugo Dyson, as J.R.R. Tolkien read aloud an early draft of *The Lord of the Rings*

I am putting a mental jigsaw together of what a hobbit looks like, based on a composite of every customer I have ever sold a copy to.

> —Shaun Bythell, *Diary of a Bookseller*

I couldn't give a damn who found the rabbit's foot or the magic mug.

> —David Hare, *The Blue Touch Paper*

I place a total embargo on dragons.
—Clive James, *Play All*

Any woman who counts on her face is a *fool*.
—Zadie Smith, *On Beauty*

Shit, I said to myself, if I stop now, I'm liable to wind up with a fucking picket fence.
—Eve Babitz, *Eve's Hollywood*

One can't build little white picket fences to keep nightmares out.
—Anne Sexton, *Paris Review* interview

In a detached house there is no one to hear you scream.
—Amanda Prowse, in *The Telegraph*

A bad review is like one of those worms in the Amazon that swims up your penis. If you read it, you can't get it out, somehow.
—Denis Johnson

It's only words, unless they're true.
—David Mamet, *Speed-the-Plow*

—And is critically acclaimed.
—Those who can't teach gym, acclaim.
—Jonathan Safran Foer, *Here I Am*

The unbelievable boredom of reviews. Has Anthony Powell had a stroke or was he always like that?

—Auberon Waugh, *The Diaries of Auberon Waugh*

Confusion hath fuck his masterpiece.

—William S. Burroughs, *Naked Lunch*

I just want to eat about a hundred million oysters and two tons of caviar and go swimming naked in champagne.

—Elaine Dundy, *The Dud Avocado*

Grace does her own shucking.

—Grace Jones's tour rider, which requests two dozen fine de claire or Colchester oysters on ice

You put your finger into it, and go swish, swish, swish.

—Jane Jacobs, on how to make a West Village martini

Wasn't the whole twentieth century a victory lap of collage, quotation, appropriation, from Picasso to Dada to Pop?

—Jonathan Lethem, *The Ecstasy of Influence*

I suddenly began to realize that everybody in America is a natural-born thief.

—Jack Kerouac, *On the Road*

The not paying for things is intoxicating.

—Philip Roth, *American Pastoral*

I don't trust anybody who hasn't shoplifted.

—John Waters

White noise about white people.

—Gil Scott-Heron, on John Knowles's A Separate Peace

Keep Britain, White.

—V. S. Naipaul's tweak of the racist slogan "Keep Britain White"

What whites called leftovers, but we knew as leavings.

—Kevin Young, "The Kitchen"

Did you know I was born in a Holiday Inn?

—Bret Easton Ellis, The Rules of Attraction

The assumptions a hotel makes about you! All the towels they give you.

—Stanley Elkin, The Dick Gibson Show

Cleanliness might not be next to godliness but it is certainly adjacent to horniness.

—Geoff Dyer, on hotels, Otherwise Known as the Human Condition

No problem is insoluble given a big enough plastic bag.

—Tom Stoppard, Jumpers

When correctly viewed
Everything is lewd.

—Tom Lehrer, "Smut"

Nothing risqué, nothing gained.
—Alexander Woollcott

The four most overrated things in life are champagne, lobster, anal sex, and picnics.
—Christopher Hitchens

[Martin Heidegger] is recorded to have laughed only once, at a picnic with Ernst Jünger in the Harz Mountains. Jünger leaned over to pick up a sauerkraut and sausage roll, and his lederhosen split with a tremendous crack.
—Paul Johnson, *Humorists*

The meat around my skull can't stop smiling.
—Catherine Lacey, *The Answers*

All of us look younger and sweeter when we smile our real smiles—the ones that come when we are genuinely happy.
—Stephen King, *From a Buick 8*

When I saw it I knew I wanted to be smiled at like that.
—Garth Greenwell, *Cleanness*

No generalization is wholly true, not even this one.
—Attributed to Benjamin Disraeli and Oliver Wendell Holmes, Jr., among others

Let's have some new clichés.
—Samuel Goldwyn

I need some new attitudes, some new affirmations and denials.

—Lionel Trilling, *Life in Culture*

There's nothing new
under the sun,
but there are new suns.

—Octavia E. Butler

It's up to you to break the old circuits.

—Hélène Cixous, *The Laugh of the Medusa*

Goodbye, and I don't mean au revoir.

—Christopher Ricks

And off he fucked.

—Kingsley Amis, attributed, after having told someone to fuck off

This is the life I've always wanted—social distancing without social disapproval.

—Tom Stoppard, on the coronavirus, in *The Spectator*

Neither am I.

—Peter Cook, responding to the boast "I'm writing a novel"

Of course it's all right for librarians to smell of drink.

—Barbara Pym, *Less Than Angels*

We courted in the style preferred by the English: alcoholically.

—Joseph O'Neill, *Netherland*

Edward worried about his drinking. Would there be enough gin? Enough ice?

    —Donald Barthelme, *Flying to America*

A big fucking bar, sis, with every kinda liquor imaginable!

    —Elaine Stritch, on what heaven will be like

No class of people are more abundantly provided with time for drinking than readers of books.

    —Delmore Schwartz, "Dostoevsky and the Bell Telephone Company"

It's all right, it's all right; everything is calm; we are just eating every thing that moves in here, dry people.

    —Barry Hannah, *Hey Jack*

My ambition was to live like music.

    —Mary Gaitskill, *Veronica*

Put thy shimmy on, Lady Chatterley!

    —D. H. Lawrence, *Lady Chatterley's Lover*

We all came into this world naked. The rest is all drag.

    —RuPaul

Treat everyone you meet like they are God in drag.

    —Baba Ram Dass

Oh honey . . . I'd love to trip through the Pentagon in heavy drag and get myself a lovely general! That would be a test of *real* democracy.

    —Charles Wright, *The Messenger*

Our own correspondent is sorry to tell
of an uneasy time, that all is not well.
>   —Wire, "Reuters"

To tell the truth, and nothing but the truth, even if the truth
is horrible.
>   —R. T. Clark, BBC home news editor, during World War II

The horror of the Twentieth Century was the size of each new
event, and the paucity of its reverberation.
>   —Norman Mailer, *Of a Fire on the Moon*

Fox News did to our parents what they thought video games
would do to us.
>   —Ryan Scott, on Twitter

I have no enemies. But my friends don't like me.
>   —Philip Larkin

There was obviously nothing to recommend me to anyone.
>   —Deborah Levy, *Hot Milk*

I have always disliked myself at any given moment; the total of
such moments is my life.
>   —Cyril Connolly, *Enemies of Promise*

I'm not much but I'm all I have.
>   —Philip K. Dick, *Martian Time-Slip*

Talk into my bullet hole. Tell me I'm fine.

—Denis Johnson, *Jesus' Son*

Every time he played a note he waved it goodbye. Sometimes he didn't even wave.

—Geoff Dyer, on Chet Baker, *But Beautiful*

I tried and I failed . . .
And I feel like going home

—Charlie Rich, "Feel Like Going Home"

Let us reflect whether there be any living writer whose silence we would consider a literary disaster.

—Cyril Connolly, *The Unquiet Grave*

If we did get a writer worth reading, should we know him when we saw him, so choked as we are with trash?

—George Orwell, *Keep the Aspidistra Flying*

Book publishing to me should be done by failed writers—editors who recognize the real thing when they see it.

—Robert Giroux, *Paris Review* interview

Books are, let's face it, better than everything else.

—Nick Hornby, *Ten Years in the Tub*

Tax *cuts* . . . for the *rich*?

—Martin Amis, *The Rub of Time*

The criminals are in the Social Register.

—George Jackson, prison interview by Jessica Mitford

Everything legal, but sinful as hell.

—Denise Giardina, *Storming Heaven*

Revenge is the capitalism of the poor.

—Aravind Adiga, *Selection Day*

It makes an immigrant laugh to hear the fears of the nationalist, scared of infection, penetration, miscegenation, when this is small fry, *peanuts*, compared to what the immigrant fears—dissolution, *disappearance*.

—Zadie Smith, *White Teeth*

The face of "evil" is always the face of total need.

—William S. Burroughs, preface to *Naked Lunch*

I've done a lot of things in my life that I haven't been proud of, but the worst thing I ever did was getting as poor as I am now.

—Richard Brautigan, *Dreaming of Babylon*

In our deepest moments we say the most inadequate things.

—Edna O'Brien, *The Love Object*

Man-o-Manischewitz!

—Buzz Aldrin, upon landing on the moon

Whatever is the plural of Applebee's?

—Roy Blount Jr., *About Three Bricks Shy: And the Load Filled Up*

I'm looking for my dignity. Don't laugh.

—Susan Sontag, *As Consciousness Is Harnessed to Flesh*

I'd rather have people ask why I have no monument than why I have one.

—Cato the Elder

Perhaps it would be a good idea for public statues to be made with disposable heads that can be changed with every change of popular fashion.

—Auberon Waugh, *The Diaries of Auberon Waugh*

I hear it was charged against me that I sought to destroy institutions.

—Walt Whitman, "I Hear It Was Charged Against Me"

May I ask for a clearer definition of "subversive activity"?

—Chelsey Minnis, "Larceny"

A government that breaks its own laws can also easily break you.

—V. S. Naipaul, *A Bend in the River*

Good-morning, Revolution: You're the very best friend I ever had.

—Langston Hughes, "Good Morning Revolution"

The purpose of a writer is to make revolution irresistible.

—Toni Cade Bambara

Sometimes a scream is better than a thesis.

> —Ralph Waldo Emerson

When you know you're going to scream . . . lay your head back, which spreads your vocal cords real wide, and when the scream comes out, it barely nicks your vocal cords.

> —Advice from the bluesman Floyd Miles, in Gregg Allman's
> *My Cross to Bear*

Let me personally give you a piece of advice. Never inhale your own vomit.

> —William Kennedy, *Ironweed*

There is nothing like puking with somebody to make you into old friends.

> —Sylvia Plath, *The Bell Jar*

A guy's not really your boyfriend until he's thrown up on you.

> —Patti Smith

Is there a hole for me to get sick in?

> —Bob Dylan, "Tombstone Blues"

Here we go . . . out of the sleep of the mild people, into the wild rippling water.

> —James Dickey, *Deliverance*

Great tracts of the Pacific Northwest . . . resembled the interior landscape of manic depression.

—Jonathan Raban, *Driving Home*

The Adirondacks are the only part of the East that Western folk respect.

—Sigrid Nunez, *Naked Sleeper*

The night before, when I had walked in to the forest at midnight, that was what I really wanted to do.

—Deborah Levy, *Things I Don't Want to Know*

We were to the woods more than once. You wanted what I wanted. It takes two to lie down, one on top of the other.

—Bernard Malamud, *The Fixer*

We must not always talk in the market-place of what happens to us in the forest.

—Nathaniel Hawthorne, *The Scarlet Letter*

Something dies when I stroll around outside.

—Richard Ford

So this is America.

—Ted Hughes, upon sleeping with Sylvia Plath for the first time

I've come to think of Europe as a hardcover book, America as the paperback version.

—Don DeLillo, *The Names*

This country is so stupid. Only spoiled white people could let something so good get so bad.

—Gary Shteyngart, *Super Sad True Love Story*

—For what purpose was the earth formed? asked Candide.
—To drive us mad, replied Martin.

—Voltaire, *Candide*

Air travel is like death: everything is taken from you.

—Elif Batuman, *The Possessed*

A picture-postcard is a symptom of loneliness.

—Graham Greene, *Our Man in Havana*

Put the coffee on, bubbles, I'm coming home.

—Richard Brautigan, *Loading Mercury with a Pitchfork*

White people couldn't cook; everybody knew that. Which made it a puzzle why such an important part of the civil rights movement had to do with integrating restaurants and lunch counters.

—Henry Louis Gates, Jr., *Colored People*

You hear a lot of jazz about soul food. The people in the ghetto want steaks. Beef steaks. I wish I had the power to see to it that the bourgeoisie really did have to make it on soul food.

—Eldridge Cleaver, *Soul on Ice*

Despite the succulent soul dinner, I did not have enough energy to masturbate.

—Charles Wright, *Absolutely Nothing to Get Alarmed About*

You shall know the truth, and the truth shall make you odd.

—Flannery O'Connor, attributed

You cannot dismiss Miss O'Connor! You cannot dismiss Miss O'Connor!

—Harry Crews, lecturing at the University of Florida

It is sweet, sometimes, to hear clichés after long days of trying to say something new.

—Patricia Lockwood, *Priestdaddy*

Oh, I love clichés!

—Paul Muldoon, *Paris Review* interview

Shit is a more onerous theological problem than is evil.

—Milan Kundera, *The Unbearable Lightness of Being*

That food was so bad I can't wait for it to become a turd and leave me.

—Thomas McGuane, *Cloudbursts*

As casual as cow-dung.

—Richard Wilbur, "Two Voices in a Meadow"

What's done is dung and cannot be undung.

—Karl Ove Knausgaard, *My Struggle: Book Five*

Enemy shit smells like the enemy.
> —A. R. Ammons, "1: The Ridge Farm"

My desire is . . . that mine adversary had written a book.
> —The Book of Job

The book of my enemy has been remaindered.
And I am pleased.
> —Clive James, "The Book of My Enemy Has Been Remaindered"

I fixed him so his unborn great-grandchildren will wet their pants
on this anniversary and not know why.
> —Robert Penn Warren, *All the King's Men*

It is my advice to anyone getting married, that they should first see
the other partner when drunk.
> —Muriel Spark, *A Far Cry from Kensington*

How dark is it legally permissible for a bar to be?
> —Harold Ross, *New Yorker* story idea

Darkness is a real fountain of youth, isn't it?
> —Karen Russell, *Orange World*

It is always darkness before delight!
> —Delmore Schwartz, "This Is a Poem I Wrote at Night, before the Dawn"

It was darker'n a carload of assholes.
> —George V. Higgins, *The Rat on Fire*

Never write "balls" with an indelible pencil on the margins of the books provided.

—Evelyn Waugh

Language is balls coming at you from every angle.

—Alan Bennett, *The Complete Talking Heads*

She began to curl her hair and long for balls.

—Jane Austen, *Northanger Abbey*

Girls have balls. They're just a little higher up.

—Joan Jett

George Washington had very large balls.

—Larry Kramer, *The American People, Volume Two*

I hear you . . . have finished a novel a hundred thousand words long consisting entirely of the word "balls" used in new groupings.

—F. Scott Fitzgerald, letter to Ernest Hemingway, *Collected Letters*

When I come out on the stage they can hear my balls clank.

—John Barrymore, on playing Hamlet

Kick him in the balls before he kicks you in yours, growled our instructor.

—E. B. Sledge, *With the Old Breed*

Doesn't this all sound balls? But it is not quite balls.

—Jean Rhys

Listen. If I wrote like that, I'd be you.

—Clive James, to an editor

Editors tend to be bad people.

—Roberto Bolaño, *Between Parentheses*

There is no editor whom I wouldn't cheerfully fry in oil.

—Ezra Pound

Dear editor: It's a damn good story. If you have any comments, write them on the back of a check.

—Erle Stanley Gardner, attributed

He who cannot howl
Will not find his pack.

—Charles Simic, "Ax"

My bulldogs are adorable, with faces like toads that have been sat on.

—Colette, letter

Reekers, leakers, smilers and defilers.

—Ambrose Bierce, on dogs

You got a life? Live it! Live the motherfuckin life!

—Toni Morrison, *Song of Solomon*

To hell with this moderation shit.

—Ai, "Boys and Girls, Lenny Bruce, or Back from the Dead"

If you can't be funny, be interesting.

—Harold Ross, on writing

If you can't be free, be a mystery.

—Rita Dove, "Canary"

If you can't be kind at least be vague.

—Judith Martin

If you aren't rich, you should always look useful.

—Louis-Ferdinand Céline

If you don't live it, it won't come out of your horn.

—Charlie Parker

If you're not nervous, you're not paying attention.

—Miles Davis

If wisdom's silence then it's time to play the fool.

—Chris Kraus, *I Love Dick*

If I can't be an ugly rumor I won't be the good time had by all.

—Bob Kaufman, "The Traveling Circus"

Motherfucking right, it's confusing.

—Chester Himes, *Blind Man with a Pistol*

Heroin to me had a nice connotation . . . Jane Eyre, Becky Sharp, Tess.

—Lucia Berlin, *A Manual for Cleaning Women*

Sometimes ah think that people become junkies just because
they subconsciously crave a wee bit ay silence.

 —Irvine Welsh, *Trainspotting*

I gave him three reasons why there were no (or very few) Jewish
junkies. Jews need eight hours of sleep. They must have fresh orange
juice in the morning. They have to read the entire N. Y. *Times*.

 —Bruce Jay Friedman, *Lucky Bruce*

I was stamped out like a Plymouth fender
into this world.

 —Anne Sexton, "Rowing"

I feel like a defective model, like I came off the assembly line
flat-out fucked.

 —Elizabeth Wurtzel, *Prozac Nation*

I knew how words worked in the way that some boys knew how
engines worked.

 —Jeanette Winterson, *Why Be Happy When You Could Be Normal?*

His body that fits with mine as if they were made in the same
body-shop.

 —Sylvia Plath, *The Unabridged Journals of Sylvia Plath*

Never trust a poet who can drive. Never trust a poet at the wheel.
If he *can* drive, distrust the poems.

 —Martin Amis, *The Information*

They had never known a woman who could swing her hips from side to side and clasp her hands to her breasts and pucker her mouth and know as much as they did about shock absorbers.

—David Plante, on Germaine Greer in a car garage, *Difficult Women*

The best mascot is a good mechanic.

—Amelia Earhart

They have strange license plates.

—Lawrence Ferlinghetti, "In Goya's Greatest Scenes We Seem to See . . ."

I love children, especially when they cry, for then someone takes them away.

—Nancy Mitford, *Decca: The Letters of Jessica Mitford*

I like children—fried.

—W. C. Fields

Bring them forth like children . . . even if they are ugly.

—Anne Sexton, on poems, *A Self-Portrait in Letters*

It made him fairly grimace, in private, to think that a child of his should be both ugly and overdressed.

—Henry James, *Washington Square*

I knew his voice was pure gold. I also knew that if anyone got a look at him he'd be dead inside of a week.

—Sam Phillips, attributed, on Roy Orbison

Ugly as death eating a dirty doughnut.

—Chuck Berry, *The Autobiography*

If I could live another forty years and spend the whole time reading, reading, reading, and learning how to write with talent . . . I would be able to blast everyone from such a big cannon that the heavens would tremble.

—Anton Chekhov, *A Life in Letters*

Go into any bookstore and try to breathe. You can't. Too many words produced by people working every morning.

—John Updike, *Bech Is Back*

The printing press could disseminate, but it could not retrieve.

—Daniel J. Boorstin, *The Discoverers*

Asking why rappers always talk about their stuff is like asking why Milton is forever listing the attributes of heavenly armies. Because boasting is a formal condition of the epic form.

—Zadie Smith, *Feel Free*

If you believe that I'm a cop killer, you believe David Bowie is an astronaut.

—Ice-T

The essential American soul is hard, isolate, stoic, and a killer.

—D. H. Lawrence

The pitter-patter of a police helicopter overhead
Looking for you.

 —Frederick Seidel, "The Ezra Pound Look-Alike"

Memory, the whole lying opera of it.

 —Barry Hannah, *Airships*

My favorite ethnic group is smart.

 —Dagoberto Gilb, interview

Intelligence is nothing without delight.

 —Paul Claudel

You've made a *blog* . . . Clever boy! Next: flushing.

 —Don Paterson, *Best Thought, Worst Thought*

The small birds twitter.

 —William Wordsworth, "Written in March"

Twitter, said Manny, waving his hand. You know what that is?
Termites with microphones.

 —Meg Wolitzer, *The Interestings*

Distracted from distraction by distraction.

 —T. S. Eliot, "Burnt Norton"

You will do foolish things, but do them with enthusiasm.

 —Colette, attributed

On the towpath we met & had to pass a long line of imbeciles . . .
They should certainly be killed.

> —Virginia Woolf, *The Diary of Virginia Woolf: Volume One, 1915–1919*

There are more kinds of fools than one can guard against.

> —Joseph Conrad, *The Secret Agent*

I've been waiting my whole life to fuck up like this.

> —Robert Stone, *Dog Soldiers*

Sometimes a mindfuck was a satisfying and productive fuck after all.

> —Meg Wolitzer, *The Interestings*

You are mine, I say to the twice-dunked cruller
before I eat it.

> —Rita Dove, "Describe Yourself in Three Words or Less"

We must have a pie. Stress cannot exist in the presence of a pie.

> —David Mamet, *Boston Marriage*

I'm as pie as is possible.

> —James Joyce, *Finnegans Wake*

The Grade A Crumpet came at him like kamikazes.

> —Clive James, on Ford Madox Ford's sex life

Very rarely guests would be considered "cake-worthy."

> —James Stourton, on Kenneth Clark

Why can't I just eat my waffle?

—Barack Obama

A happy childhood has spoiled many a promising life.

—Robertson Davies

Unless carefree, motherlove was a killer.

—Toni Morrison, *Beloved*

It was Diane's view that bringing up a completely undamaged child was in bad taste.

—Rachel Cusk, *Transit*

I was being fucked up, at last, by choice.

—Ocean Vuong, *On Earth We're Briefly Gorgeous*

Wanting to meet an author because you like his work is like wanting to meet a duck because you like pâté.

—Margaret Atwood, quoting another writer

No animal likes to be pecked on the anus by a duck.

—Nicholson Baker, *A Box of Matches*

There, but for a typographical error, is the story of my life.

—Dorothy Parker, on ducking for apples, in *The Uncollected Dorothy Parker*

One melancholy lesson of advancing years is the realization that you can't make old friends.

—Christopher Hitchens, in *Harper's Magazine*

What can you do with a friend? You can't fuck him.

—William Carlos Williams

We don't want to fuck each other and we don't know each other well enough to have comfortable silences, so we have to talk.

—T. Gertler, *Elbowing the Seducer*

Say your life broke down. The last good kiss
you had was years ago.

—Richard Hugo, "Degrees of Gray in Philipsburg"

Despair came over her, as it will when nobody around has any sexual relevance to you.

—Thomas Pynchon, *The Crying of Lot 49*

Under what circumstances can you imagine sleeping with me? Global apocalypse? National pandemic?

—Karen Russell, *Vampires in the Lemon Grove*

One test of *un homme sérieux* is that it is possible to learn from him even when one radically disagrees with him.

—Christopher Hitchens, *And Yet*

The basic ecology of literary life [is] that if you are not sometimes attacked, then you cannot be very good.

—John Gregory Dunne, *Crooning*

If you can't annoy somebody . . . there's little point in writing.

—Kingsley Amis

Try me, you post-print punk.

> —John Updike, *Bech Is Back*

—I'm reviewing it, the stooped man said, and started to plod off.
—You read it?
—No, he said over his shoulder, but I know the son of a bitch
  who wrote it.

> —William Gaddis, *The Recognitions*

Precancer? . . . Isn't that . . . like life?

> —Lorrie Moore, *Like Life*

In fiction, it's never benign.

> —Rebecca Schiff, *The Bed Moved*

The orchestra was just finishing the formless waltz of the syphilitic
prostitute.

> —Terry Southern and Mason Hoffenberg, *Candy*

The oboe pungent as a bitch in heat.

> —James Merrill, "The Victor Dog"

You never dreamed, did you, that a piano could be made to express
all that?

> —Marcel Proust, *In Search of Lost Time*

Do you try to listen to classical music but feel you don't ever really
advance past knowing it's better than it sounds?

> —Padgett Powell, *The Interrogative Mood*

Take deads
Away.
Play music
Please.

—J. P. Donleavy, *The Ginger Man*

The thing that stood between me and murder was always a
buzzsaw guitar.

—Donna Gaines, *A Misfit's Manifesto*

We're all one beat away from becoming elevator music.

—Don DeLillo, *Paris Review* interview

How desperate do you have to be to start doing push-ups to solve
your problems?

—Karl Ove Knausgaard, *My Struggle: Book Two*

A brown condom full of walnuts.

—Clive James, describing Arnold Schwarzenegger

If we are to be fried alive, it seems funny to be working out.

—Christopher Isherwood, *The Sixties: Diaries 1960–1969*

Does breakfast in bed count as a morning workout?

—Elizabeth Jane Howard

Caffeine was my exercise.

—Ottessa Moshfegh, *My Year of Rest and Relaxation*

Intellectual arses wobble the best.

—Harold Pinter, *Mountain Language*

Fleas dream about buying a dog.

—Eduardo Galeano, *Border Crossing*

When a man's best friend is his dog, that dog has a problem.

—Edward Abbey, attributed

If you are totally alone I suppose it's quite a comfort to have a dumb friend lurking.

—William Rushton, *Super Pig*

Think about this. All the little animals of your youth are long dead.

—Charles Portis, *The Dog of the South*

Critical essays are really where it's at.

—Jim Morrison

I can't read any more of this Rich Critical Prose,
he growled, broke wind, and scratched himself & left
that fragrant area.

—John Berryman, "Dream Song 170"

Be light, stinging, insolent, and melancholy.

—Words hanging over Kenneth Tynan's desk

So much thought about everything appears in the form of literary criticism.

—Iris Murdoch, *Living on Paper: Letters from Iris Murdoch, 1934–1995*

Whatever they criticize you for, intensify it.

—Jean Cocteau

Of all reviews, the crushing review is the most popular, as being the most readable.

—Anthony Trollope, *The Way We Live Now*

Let me give you my feedback. My feedback is arf arf arf.

—Chelsey Minnis, "Nerves"

Here is a wonderful and delightful thing, that we should have furnished ourselves with orifices.

—Rose Macaulay, "Eating and Drinking"

Can I get more orifices? . . . The three on offer aren't enough to sustain a marriage.

—Nell Zink, *The Wallcreeper*

I shall probably discover residual traces of a Mars bar in his anus.

—Angela Carter, letter

Whenever a thing is done for the first time, it releases a little demon.

—Emily Dickinson

If this was love, love had been overrated.

—Henry James, *The Europeans*

I am crazy about being drunk. I like it like Patton liked war.
—James Dickey

I got deflowered on two cans of Rainier Ale when I was 17 . . . I began
to wonder what else there was out there that was like Rainier Ale.
—Eve Babitz, *Eve's Hollywood*

When the beer came, I dipped a finger in it and wet down each
corner of the paper napkin to anchor it, so it would not come up
with the mug each time and make me appear ridiculous.
—Charles Portis, *The Dog of the South*

My dad was the town drunk. Usually that's not so bad, but New
York City?
—Henny Youngman

Turn on, tune in, drop out, fuck up, crawl back.
—Grover Lewis

I'm quite illiterate, but I read a lot.
—J. D. Salinger, *The Catcher in the Rye*

I'm partial to anyone who looks half blind.
—Gary Shteyngart, *Absurdistan*

I love to read the way people love to watch television.
—Susan Sontag, *Rolling Stone* interview

I enjoy vegetarian food the way I enjoy a kick in the stomach.
—Roberto Bolaño, *Between Parentheses*

There is apparently a causal link between heroin addiction and
vegetarianism.

 —Irvine Welsh, *Trainspotting*

Eating celery like crazy, because someone said Kinsey discovered
it was the only thing for potency.

 —Christopher Isherwood, *The Sixties: Diaries 1960–1969*

The only thing that I hate more intensely than melodrama and
spinach is myself.

 —Saul Bellow, *Letters*

We don't want nutrition, we want taste.

 —Alice B. Toklas, attributed

People feel so special, so wise, when somebody they know
drops dead.

 —Ottessa Moshfegh, *Homesick for Another World*

I have certainly rounded third base and am headed for home plate,
which is a hole in the ground.

 —Jim Harrison, *The Beast God Forgot to Invent*

Don't grieve for the dead: they know what they're doing.

 —Clarice Lispector, *The Hour of the Star*

I didn't kill him, I just fucked him.

 —Toni Morrison, *Sula*

I don't fuck white guys, but if I had to fuck a white guy, I'd fuck you.

—Susan Choi, *Trust Exercise*

DECOLONISE YOUR PUSSY.

—Coffee mug in Namwali Serpell's *The Old Drift*

We must always be on guard against mediocre cussing in our writing.

—Katherine Dunn, *On Cussing*

Let's get in the same racket.
The racket is dirty talk.

—Chelsey Minnis, "Larceny"

I flat ran over Dreamer Tatum, cunt on cunt.

—Dan Jenkins, *Semi-Tough*

Some girl who got around started calling me "Wondercunt."

—Eve Babitz, *Eve's Hollywood*

The best time to drink champagne is before lunch, you cunt.

—Harold Pinter, *No Man's Land*

The cold cunt of reality.

—Charles Wright, *Absolutely Nothing to Get Alarmed About*

Better to have been a dickhead and seen it,
than be a cunt all your life and not know it.

—Kate Tempest, "These things I know"

Russell Ash found a whole family of Cunts living in England in the nineteenth century.

—Kate Lister, *A Curious History of Sex*

He paces up and down like one of those fuckin Inspector Morse type of cunts.

—Irvine Welsh, *Filth*

I walked over and started grabbing at cheese, pickled-pigs' feet and chicken cunt.

—Charles Bukowski, *Tales of Ordinary Madness*

Fucking, cunting, bloody good.

—Philip Larkin, on Sidney Bechet's music

I like how shocked people are when you say "cunt." It's like I have a nuclear bomb in my underpants.

—Caitlin Moran, *How to Be a Woman*

Shall we go to the cunt?

—Lady Caroline Blackwood, speaking of the country

In certain trying circumstances . . . profanity furnishes a relief denied even to prayer.

—Mark Twain

My message to the world is Fuck it!

—John O'Hara, 1934 letter to F. Scott Fitzgerald

My knowledge of the world consisted of fucking hell, fucking hell, fucking hell.

—Anna Burns, *Milkman*

Fuck humanity, was my basic position at that point.

—Hari Kunzru, *White Tears*

The sky is low—the clouds are mean.

—Emily Dickinson

Look how black the sky is, the writer said. *I made it that way.*

—Bret Easton Ellis, *Lunar Park*

Don't say what you would or wouldn't do, honey. Cause one day you might have to.

—Larry Brown, *Fay*

Be careful what you say. It comes true. It comes true.

—Maxine Hong Kingston, *The Woman Warrior*

Don't let your mouth start nothing that your ass can't stand.

—Toni Morrison, *Sula*

If you bare your arse to a vengeful unicorn, the number of possible outcomes dwindles to one.

—David Mitchell, *The Bone Clocks*

And you told me I wouldn't need my arse helmet.

—Susan Choi, *Trust Exercise*

My arse isn't right since the octopus we ate in Málaga.

—Kevin Barry, *Night Boat to Tangier*

You have played enough; you have eaten and drunk enough.
It's time you went home.

—Horace

Go—and never darken my towels again.

—Groucho Marx, in *Duck Soup*

Superior people never make long visits.

—Marianne Moore, "Silence"

Your back is my favorite part of you,
the part furthest away from your mouth.

—Louise Glück, "Purple Bathing Suit"

You must come again when you have less time.

—Walter Sickert

My daughter says to her friends "a mother is someone who types
all day."

—Anne Sexton, *A Self-Portrait in Letters*

No one can write with a child around.

—Doris Lessing

I used to not be able to work if there were dishes in the sink. Then
I had a child and now I can work if there is a corpse in the sink.

—Anne Lamott

If Anything Will Level with You Water Will.

—A. R. Ammons, poem title

Swimming, like dying, seems to solve all problems: and you remain alive.

—Iris Murdoch

I took the lake between my legs.

—Maxine Kumin, "Morning Swim"

To care for the quarrels of the past . . . is rare in America.

—Mary McCarthy, *Memories of a Catholic Girlhood*

The United States of Amnesia.

—Gore Vidal

This is what history consists of. It's the sum total of all the things they aren't telling us.

—Don DeLillo, *Libra*

There are fuckers and fuckees.

—John Lennon

The Archangel took his role of fucker seriously.

—Jean Genet, *Our Lady of the Flowers*

This was the world they were meant to enter: a world of fuckers.

—Meg Wolitzer, *The Interestings*

Everyone is in the best seat.

—John Cage

Seat all the bores together . . . They don't realize they're the bores, and they're happy.

> —Lady Elizabeth Anson

The "gristle" seat.

> —Sally Quinn, on the seat between two bores, *The Party*

I ask the gentleman on my right, Are you a bed-wetter? And when we have exhausted that, I remark to the gentleman on my left, You know, I spit blood this morning.

> —Virginia Faulkner, on dealing with bores

Do you like string?

> —Jerry Wadsworth, final attempt to elicit a response from a dull dinner partner

Did you know you can trick people into being more interesting by being more interesting yourself?

> —Elisa Gabbert, "New Theories on Boredom"

I want one Falstaff for every Hal.

> —Tina Brown, on dinner parties, *The Vanity Fair Diaries*

It wasn't clarity I was after. I wanted things to be less clear.

> —Deborah Levy, *Hot Milk*

Self-knowledge is always bad news.

> —John Barth, *Giles Goat-Boy*

A Hong Kong meal . . . is a statement to which customers are secondary.
　　—Food writer quoted by Kingsley Amis

I know that sort of meal, and the statement is Fuck You, and you haven't got to go to Hong Kong for it. Soho is far enough.
　　—Kingsley Amis, in reply

Thank you for your invitation to host a fundraising dinner in the private room of a top London restaurant. I would rather die.
　　—Harold Pinter

I say as Epicurus said, that a man should not so much respect what he eateth, as with whom he eateth.
　　— Michel de Montaigne, *Essays*

Another big eater was Chou Yi-han of Changchow, who fried a ghost.
　　—Maxine Hong Kingston, *The Woman Warrior*

I have eaten many strange things, but have never eaten the heart of a king before.
　　—Augustus J. C. Hare, *The Story of My Life*

You ever cook any Devil brains yourself? Don't knock it if you haven't tried it.
　　—R. A. Lafferty, *Past Master*

I would rather feel your spine than your skull, whoever you are.
　　—Herman Melville, *Moby-Dick*

Oh, Jesus, female sexuality is a cruel cross to bear!
—Angela Carter, journal

There were 117 psychoanalysts on the Pan Am flight to Vienna and
I'd been treated by at least six of them.
—Erica Jong, *Fear of Flying*

Which flight had he been on? the red eye or brown nose?
—Joshua Cohen, *Book of Numbers*

He has a morbid fear of missing airplanes, and of being dropped
from the tail-end lavatory.
—John Updike, *Bech: A Book*

The cry of an angel falling backward through an open window.
—Dwight Yoakam, on Roy Orbison's voice

A friend of mine once observed that you could recognize a Katz if
it fell out of an airplane at 30,000 feet.
—David Salle, on Alex Katz, *How to See*

Bring me the sunset in a cup.
—Emily Dickinson

That sunburnt feeling is moving inside of me, like light breaking in
double time over the crops.
—Greg Jackson, on bourbon, *Prodigals*

I don't like an empty house at sunset.
>   —Ann Fleming

I don't know any writers who don't drink.
>   —James Baldwin

Nurse . . . you have a lovely pitching arm.
>   —Said to a bartender in Denis Johnson's *Jesus' Son*

The object of life is to make sure you die a weird death.
>   —Thomas Pynchon, *Gravity's Rainbow*

—Die young and leave a beautiful corpse. Who said that?
—Someone who liked fucking corpses.
>   —Ottessa Moshfegh, *My Year of Rest and Relaxation*

We are low on marmalade.
>   —Last words of Lord Grimthorpe

Publishers needed favorable reviews . . . as an Easter basket needs shredded green paper.
>   —Elizabeth Hardwick, *The Collected Essays of Elizabeth Hardwick*

Both Lizzieites and anti-Lizzieites were disposed to think that Lizzie was very clever.
>   —Anthony Trollope, *The Eustace Diamonds*

This is just the book to give your sister if she's a loud, dirty, boozy girl.
>   —Dylan Thomas, blurbing Flann O'Brien's At *Swim-Two-Birds*

It had never occurred to me that book reviews might be written week after week chiefly in order to make the reading of books unnecessary.

 —Delmore Schwartz, "An Author's Brother-in-Law"

To overpraise is a subtle form of disrespect—and everybody knows it.

 —Mary Gaitskill, *Somebody with a Little Hammer*

Giddy chorus girls just waiting to be fucked.

 —Alan Bennett, on too-nice theater critics, in *The Guardian*

I still get a thrill every time the curtain goes up.

 —Kenneth Tynan

I get a thrill every time it goes down.

 —Clive James, on why he never wrote theater criticism

There are few things more abrasive to the human spirit, even in Patagonia, than someone standing behind you chomping and sucking ice cubes.

 —Paul Theroux, *The Old Patagonian Express*

God, humans are a noisy zoo—
especially educated ones armed with *vin rouge*
and an incomprehensible no-act play.

 —Rita Dove, "Persephone in Hell"

—How many performance artists does it take to screw in a
   light bulb?
—I don't know. I left early.
   —Lynne Tillman, *No Lease on Life*

I am afraid, this morning, of my face.
   —Randall Jarrell, "Next Day"

Sometimes you get a flash of what you look like to other people.
   —Zadie Smith, *On Beauty*

It's very difficult to feel contempt for others when you see yourself
in the mirror.
   —Harold Pinter, interview

No one ever tells you the truth about what you look like.
   —Rachel Cusk, *Transit*

—My sister has just returned from a week's holiday in Paris, and,
   do you know, she didn't go to the Louvre once.
—Good lord, change of food, I expect.
   —Joke in *Dylan Thomas: The Collected Letters*

The burden of keeping three people in toilet paper seemed to me
rather a heavy one.
   —Barbara Pym, *Excellent Women*

I loathe my belly, that trunkful of bowels . . . or else indigestion with a first installment of hot filth pouring out of me in a public toilet.

 —Vladimir Nabokov, *The Original of Laura*

He tore away half the prize story sharply and wiped himself with it.

 —James Joyce, *Ulysses*

All my good reading, you might say, was done in the toilet.

 —Henry Miller, *Black Spring*

If I need any shit from you, I'll squeeze your head.

 —Kris Kristofferson, to Jon Peters

What contempt the people who think up souvenirs have for other people.

 —Diane Johnson, *Natural Opium*

That the native does not like the tourist is not hard to explain.

 —Jamaica Kincaid, *A Small Place*

Saigon. *Shit.*

 —Martin Sheen, in *Apocalypse Now*

I was ready to infiltrate Hanoi, grab Uncle Ho by the goatee, pull off his face, and make a clean escape.

 —Thom Jones, *Sonny Liston Was a Friend of Mine*

STREETS FLOODED. PLEASE ADVISE.

>—Robert Benchley, telegram from Venice

Fuck them for getting to live in a place like this.

>—Garth Greenwell, on Venice, *Cleanness*

That profuse upstairs delicatessen of mine.

>—Seymour Krim, on his memory, *Missing a Beat: The Rants and Regrets of Seymour Krim*

Closing the bodega down for real.

>—Cy Twombly, on death, in Sally Mann's *Hold Still*

Disintegration—I'm taking it in stride.

>—Bret Easton Ellis, *American Psycho*

I am so half an orange without you.

>—Anne Sexton, *A Self-Portrait in Letters*

They are very nice to eat, oranges, when you've been having sex for ages. They cut through the fug and smell very organised.

>—Claire-Louise Bennett, *Pond*

—Mother, how many pips in a tangerine?
—Shut up, you little bastard.

>—Dylan Thomas, *The Collected Letters*

Is there a nemesis in the house?

>—Stanley Elkin, *The Dick Gibson Show*

I don't care if people hate my guts; I assume most of them do. The important question is whether they are in a position to do anything about it.

—William S. Burroughs

—There are so few areas of transcendence left.
—Don't forget the languid contemplation of the miseries of others.

—Robert Jay Lifton and Christopher Hitchens

People seldom read a book which is given to them.

—Samuel Johnson

I turned another page in the book although I hadn't read the previous one.

—Sally Rooney, *Conversations with Friends*

A man who has not read Homer is like a man who has never seen the ocean.

—Walter Bagehot

Life is slow suicide, unless you read.

—Herman Wouk, *The Caine Mutiny*

Thank God for books as an alternative to conversation.

—W. H. Auden

There are no nineteenth century ballads about being gay.

—Colm Tóibín

Relax, Amy, I'm not gay . . . I just like Sleater-Kinney.

 —Emily Gould, *Friendship*

Just because I like to suck cock doesn't make me any less American than Jesse Helms.

 —Allen Ginsberg

You can't work in a haberdashery in the sticks without knowing what a fairy is.

 —Larry Kramer, *The American People: Volume One*

I once started out
to walk around the world
but ended up in Brooklyn.
That Bridge was just too much for me.

 —Lawrence Ferlinghetti, *A Coney Island of the Mind*

Is Brooklyn itself a geographical form of insanity?

 —Jonathan Lethem, *The Fortress of Solitude*

What business is it of yours where I'm from, friendo?

 —Cormac McCarthy, *No Country for Old Men*

Who goes there? hankering, gross, mystical and nude?

 —Walt Whitman, "Song of Myself"

Your gross body my favorite song.

 —Danez Smith, "Acknowledgments"

The naked person always has the social advantage over the
clothed one.

  —Alan Hollinghurst, *The Swimming-Pool Library*

You were naked. I'm a sucker for the first person singular.

  —Stanley Elkin, *The Dick Gibson Show*

Man, there she stood without her anthropology on!

  —Ralph Ellison, *The Selected Letters of Ralph Ellison*

More of this sitting around like beasts!

  —W. H. Auden

I have a lifelong horror of sandy beaches.

  —Harold Bloom, *Possessed by Memory*

—You know what people who go to nude beaches look like?
—Tell me.
—People who shouldn't go to nude beaches.

  —Elmore Leonard, *Be Cool*

Who is there that abstains from reading that which is printed in
abuse of himself?

  —Anthony Trollope, *Phineas Finn*

Let me never fall into the vulgar mistake of dreaming that I am
persecuted whenever I am contradicted.

  —Ralph Waldo Emerson, journals

Injustice is relatively easy to bear; what stings is justice.

> —H. L. Mencken

Bones heal, pain is temporary and chicks dig scars.

> —Evel Knievel, attributed

I have scars on my hands from touching certain people.

> —J. D. Salinger, *Raise High the Roof Beam, Carpenters*

Many's the long night I've dreamed of cheese—toasted, mostly.

> —Robert Louis Stevenson, *Treasure Island*

White people eat cheese for breakfast and smell of it all day.

> —Aravind Adiga, *Selection Day*

Fuck cheese. Cheese is all about spores, and, and molds and all that shit. Maybe cheese is trying to colonize our brains.

> —Michael Chabon, *Telegraph Avenue*

No wine, she said. It leads to cheese.

> —Lorrie Moore, *Bark*

Every normal man must be tempted, at times, to spit on his hands, hoist the black flag, and begin slitting throats.

> —H. L. Mencken

The old ultra-violence.

> —Anthony Burgess, *A Clockwork Orange*

Oh, I'm not a percussionist, I just like to hit things.

> —Tom Waits

Things mount up inside one, and then one has to perpetrate an outrage.

—Muriel Spark, *Robinson*

Don't confuse honors with achievement.

—Zadie Smith

Literature has nothing to do with national prizes and everything to do with a strange rain of blood, sweat, semen, and tears.

—Roberto Bolaño, *Between Parentheses*

Not only should you not accept a prize. You should not try to deserve one either.

—Jean Cocteau, attributed

Prizes are for parents so they'll know.

—Anne Sexton, *A Self-Portrait in Letters*

Honey, no offense, but sometimes I think I could shoot you and watch you kick.

—Raymond Carver, *Where I'm Calling From*

If you're ever angry enough to hit somebody, don't do it. Cool down and get yourself a pistol.

—Elmore Leonard, *Maximum Bob*

You know, there's a distinct lack of female arms dealers, I've always thought.

—Sally Rooney, *Conversations with Friends*

Guns . . . were invented by boys who had never gotten over their disappointment that accompanying their own orgasm there wasn't a big *boom* sound.

—Lorrie Moore, *Like Life*

I am a bullet, being shot out of a dirty gun.

—Caitlin Moran, *How to Build a Girl*

She was already a missile, armed and targeted.

—Octavia E. Butler, *Parable of the Talents*

The vote . . . means nothing to women, we should be armed.

—Edna O'Brien, *The Country Girls*

Every woman should have a blowtorch.

—Julia Child, attributed

Cookery means the knowledge of Medea and of Circe and of Helen and of the Queen of Sheba.

—John Ruskin

As for the Queen of Sheba, I doubt she ever made so much as a piece of toast.

—Margaret Atwood, *The Blind Assassin*

I think women admire Marlene Dietrich so much because she looks as if she ate men whole, for breakfast, possibly on toast.

—Angela Carter

Come out, my eight-slice beauty.

> —Ann Beattie, on a toaster given as a Christmas gift,
> *The Burning House*

Mother doesn't cook, Ignatius said dogmatically. She burns.

> —John Kennedy Toole, *A Confederacy of Dunces*

Her favourite food is anything burnt.

> —Ali Smith, *Spring*

Every grain of rice you leave behind is one maggot you eat in hell.

> —Ocean Vuong, *On Earth We're Briefly Gorgeous*

You know, massa, Bugs Bunny wasn't nothing but Br'er Rabbit with a better agent.

> —Paul Beatty, *The Sellout*

God created black people and black people created style.

> —George C. Wolfe, *The Colored Museum*

I'm as American as apple pie. But no. I cannot, simply cannot, don a mask and suck the c— of that sweet, secure bitch, middle-class American life.

> —Charles Wright, *The Messenger*

Just one hog ass thing *after* the other.

> —Albert Murray, on being black, *The Omni-Americans*

He that drinks his cider alone, let him catch his horse alone.

> —Benjamin Franklin

In victory you deserve champagne. In defeat you need it.

—Napoleon Bonaparte, attributed

Twit twit twit
Jug jug jug jug jug jug.

—T. S. Eliot, *The Waste Land*

One can only pour out of a jug that which is in it.

—Anthony Trollope, *Framley Parsonage*

A well-minxed martini.

—Kevin Young, "The Suspects"

No martini, no lecture.

—Dean Acheson, warning to the Brookings Institution

A young girl's voice. She is dressed in a nun's habit. The boy turns
and faces her. She proffers a chalice of cervical exudate and he
drinks from it.

—Nick Tosches, start of a review of Black Sabbath's *Paranoid*,
    in *Rolling Stone*

Questions arose. Like, what in the fuck was going on here, basically.

—Thomas Pynchon, *Inherent Vice*

Oh, man, this is wyrd.

—N. Scott Momaday, "Death Comes for Beowulf"

The mind that is not baffled is not employed.

—Wendell Berry

There's nothing you can't fuck up if you try hard enough.

—Nick Hornby, *A Long Way Down*

Canadians. Grrr!

—Iris Murdoch, *Living on Paper*

Canadians, do not vomit on me!

—Elizabeth Hardwick, *Sleepless Nights*

I dreamed that I threw up a fox.

—Joy Williams, "The Visiting Privilege"

Puking overboard to feed the herrings.

—James Joyce, *Ulysses*

—Don't you think that a comic book about Auschwitz is in bad taste?

—No, I thought Auschwitz was in bad taste.

—Art Spiegelman, interview about *Maus*

There is no more beautiful a sight, he said, than to see a fine woman bashing away at a typewriter.

—Muriel Spark, *The Ballad of Peckham Rye*

Teabags, Tampax and the *TLS*.

—Angela Carter's description of Lorna Sage's house

She loved to walk down the street with a book under her arm.
It had the same significance for her as an elegant cane for a dandy
a century ago.

—Milan Kundera, *The Unbearable Lightness of Being*

I wished critics would judge me as an author, not as a woman.

—Charlotte Brontë

Just because I'm so wretchedly plain doesn't mean I can do
without things.

—William Trevor, "Flights of Fancy"

Plain women know more about men than beautiful women do.

—Katharine Hepburn, attributed

Why was "plain" a euphemism for "ugly"?

—Elif Batuman, *The Idiot*

You might pass Eleanor Harding in the street without notice, but
you could hardly pass an evening with her and not lose your heart.

—Anthony Trollope, *The Warden*

I may look like a beer salesman, but I'm a poet.

—Theodore Roethke

Any person with small sharp features that are bunched in the
center of his face can be expected to be called a rat about three
times a year.

—Charles Portis, *The Dog of the South*

The January issue is suddenly so full of people with bald heads,
I had to kill three of them today.

    —Tina Brown, *The Vanity Fair Diaries*

Head shaved clean as a porn star's testicle.

    —Michael Chabon, *Telegraph Avenue*

You must not mind me, madam; I say strange things, but I mean
no harm.

    —Samuel Johnson

If you feel strange, strange things will happen to you.

    —Rita Dove, "Best Western Motor Lodge, AAA Approved"

—I've got an FFF inside.
—What's that, sir?
—A fucking funny feeling.

    —Deborah Levy, *Swimming Home*

That's what being alive's all about, all those fucked up feelings.
You've got to have them; when you stop, watch out.

    —Irvine Welsh, *The Acid House*

Forgetting that one should never answer the telephone in a dream,
I take a call.

    —Don Paterson, *Best Thought, Worst Thought*

Who hasn't woken up screaming in a four-poster elephant herd?

—Paul Muldoon, "The Side Project"

Reality had always been something of an unknown quantity to me.

—Anna Kavan, *Ice*

A dream is just a nightmare with lipstick.

—Toni Morrison, *Love*

If you're sad or heartbroken, make yourself up, dress up, add more lipstick and attack.

—Coco Chanel, attributed

He did secretly pine for an extra dictionary "label": namely, *illit.*, to go with *colloq.* and *derog.* and the rest.

—Martin Amis, on Kingsley Amis, *The Rub of Time*

This erratum slip has been inserted by mistake.

—Alasdair Gray, *Unlikely Stories, Mostly*

Don't cite dictionaries to me . . . Dictionary people consult me, not I them.

—John O'Hara

Folks don't necessarily have to be able to use all them big dictionary words to understand life.

—Albert Murray, *South to a Very Old Place*

He has never been known to use a word that might cause the reader to check with a dictionary.

—William Faulkner, on Ernest Hemingway

Poor Faulkner. Does he really think big emotions come from big words?

> —Ernest Hemingway, on William Faulkner

There ain't a woman in the world who ain't a fool for a talking bit.

> —Record producer Billy Sherrill, to Elvis Costello, *Unfaithful Music and Disappearing Ink*

Ah, I perceive what you are about! You are turning this whole affair into a ballad.

> —Nathaniel Hawthorne, *The Blithedale Romance*

When Johnny Rotten rolled his r's, it sounded as if his teeth had been ground down to points.

> —Greil Marcus, *Lipstick Traces*

Writers, like teeth, are divided into incisors and grinders.

> —Walter Bagehot

All my clothes had holes in them from where the sensors had been attached.

> —Rachel Kushner, *The Mars Room*

A hole in your sock may have just occurred; not so with a darn.

> —Lord Chesterfield, *Lord Chesterfield's Letters*

Wind, rain, work, and mockery were his tailors.

> —Walker Evans, on James Agee

—Lots of fellows have asked me who my tailor is.

—Doubtless in order to avoid him, sir.

> —P. G. Wodehouse, "Jeeves Takes Charge"

Fashion is about long black cars when you need them.

> —Liz Tilberis

What I like about limousines is that they have tinted windows, so no-one can see if you're snogging in the back seat.

> —Elizabeth Jane Howard

The Trojans never did any harm to *me*.

> —Achilles, in Homer's *The Iliad*

I ain't got no quarrel with them Vietcong.

> —Muhammad Ali

I would give all my profound Greek to dance really well.

> —Virginia Woolf

God match me with a good dancer!

> —William Shakespeare, *Much Ado About Nothing*

Verily thou shakest a wicked ankle.

> —Zora Neale Hurston, *Hitting a Straight Lick with a Crooked Stick*

What man would not be a dancer if he could.

> —Cormac McCarthy, *Blood Meridian*

I have actually been written up in columns as "the best dancer among the literati."
  —John O'Hara, *Selected Letters of John O'Hara*

The body says what words cannot.
  —Martha Graham

I'm so afraid she's going to give birth to a cube on stage.
  —Stark Young, on Martha Graham

Almost nobody dances sober, unless they happen to be insane.
  —H. P. Lovecraft

He who fusses about a mosquito net can never hope to dance with a goat.
  —Vaclav Havel, *The Garden Party*

I will *gnat* sleep in that room again.
  —Elizabeth Barrett, diary

—I get out of bed and throw up and take a shower and shave and have breakfast.
—You throw up *every* morning?
—Of course, doesn't everyone?
  —E. J. Kahn, in conversation with a surprised Brendan Gill

The hangover became a part of the day as well allowed-for as the Spanish siesta.

—F. Scott Fitzgerald, *The Crack-Up*

Besides my conscience, my liver was the most abused part of my body.

—Viet Thanh Nguyen, *The Sympathizer*

The floor seemed wonderfully solid. It was comforting to know I had fallen and could fall no further.

—Sylvia Plath, *The Bell Jar*

He resolved, having done it once, never to move his eyeballs again.

—Kingsley Amis, on a hangover, *Lucky Jim*

If you keep drinking your babies will come out crosseyed, and you'll end up buried in a strange town with your name spelled wrong on your grave.

—Denis Johnson, *The Largesse of the Sea Maiden*

Lead me not into Penn Station.

—Saul Bellow, *Herzog*

Penn Station, a place so filthy, confused, and depressing that even the pimps and whores can't stand it.

—Robert Hughes, *The Spectacle of Skill*

One entered the city like a god. One scuttles in now like a rat.

—Vincent Scully, on old versus new Penn Station

When you played there you sounded like the Knicks.

—Gil Scott-Heron, on Madison Square Garden, *The Last Holiday*

How thrilling it would be, if only one couldn't read!

—G. K. Chesterton, on Times Square

And you, stand-up lady, are golden as the sun.

—Norman Mailer, letter to Norris Church Mailer

Why had I been so consumed by this old, fat, bombastic, lying little dynamo?

—Norris Church Mailer, on Norman Mailer, *A Ticket to the Circus*

Say, who among us does not care to be undressed?

—August Kleinzahler, "The Dog Stoltz"

Prithee, undo this button.

—Lord Byron, *Letters and Journals of Lord Byron*

Pluck me whilst I blush!

—James Joyce, *Finnegans Wake*

There's no nature in New York and the closest you can get is an orgasm.

—Jim Harrison, *The Beast God Forgot to Invent*

Integrity is the orgasm.

—Doris Lessing

Many men wanted to lay me down. But few wanted to pick me up.
> —Eartha Kitt

I only know that people call me a feminist whenever I express sentiments that differentiate me from a doormat.
> —Dame Rebecca West

What I wanted . . . was everything.
> —Eve Babitz, *Eve's Hollywood*

William Faulkner walks into a bar.
Bartender: Why the long phrase?
> —Overheard

He sharpens my zest for writing, that man.
> —Iris Murdoch, on Faulkner, *Living on Paper*

There's that line that Faulkner said, about how you don't love *because*. You love *despite*.
> —Meg Wolitzer, *The Female Persuasion*

One Willyam ass goddam Faulkner, peckerwood, whom I repeat *rigoureusement*, watch, can write his old Mississippi peckerwood ass off.
> —Albert Murray, *South to a Very Old Place*

I will call a turd a turd and our boy is pretty full these days.
> —Ralph Ellison to Albert Murray, on Faulkner, *Trading Twelves: The Selected Letters of Ralph Ellison and Albert Murray*

It is the destiny of mint to be crushed.
—Waverley Root

If dolphins tasted good, he said, we wouldn't even know about
their language.
—Lorrie Moore, *Bark*

That pale porpoise and his plush vulgarities.
—Vladimir Nabokov, on Henry James

Why do sole and turbot borrow the colors and even the contours
of the sea bottom? Out of self-protection? No, out of self-disgust.
—Cyril Connolly, *The Unquiet Grave*

Three films a day, three books a week and records of great music
would be enough to make me happy to the day I die.
—François Truffaut

After four movies, three concerts, and two-and-a-half museums,
you sleep with him. It seems the right number of cultural events.
—Lorrie Moore, "How to Be an Other Woman"

I don't like the feeling that I know men who go to shows in the
afternoon. It's worse than smoking reefers.
—Harold Ross, *Letters from the Editor*

I am a whole theater unto myself.
—Mary Ellen Pleasant, in *Pandex of the Press*

Happiness is a monstrosity; they who seek it are punished.

—Gustave Flaubert, *The Letters of Gustave Flaubert: 1830–1857*

Happy as a clam, is what my mother says for happy. I am happy as a clam: hardshelled, firmly closed.

—Margaret Atwood, *Cat's Eye*

Old southern graveyards harbor an unwholesome power comparable to that of nuclear disaster sites.

—Denis Johnson, *The Largesse of the Sea Maiden*

Jesus, the South is fine, isn't it. It's better than the theatre, isn't it. It's better than Ben Hur, isn't it.

—William Faulkner, *Absalom, Absalom*

Only the music got away clean.

—Greil Marcus, on Southern culture, *Mystery Train*

A lot of people leave Arkansas and most of them come back sooner or later. They can't quite achieve escape velocity.

—Charles Portis, *Dog of the South*

Somebody's boring me. I think it's me.

—Dylan Thomas

If I ever bore you it'll be with a knife.

—Louise Brooks

You can be bored with anything if you try hard enough.

—Samuel R. Delany, *Nova*

Proust, James, Voltaire, Donne, Lucretius—how we would have
bored them!

> —Cyril Connolly, *The Unquiet Grave*

If it were read in the open air, birds would fall stunned from
the sky.

> —Clive James, on the boredom of Nikita Khrushchev's memoirs

I jerked off
driving home alone one-handed.

> —John Updike, "Midpoint"

It's done with a flick of the wrist.

> —Bob Dylan, "Sweetheart Like You"

Foreskins come and foreskins go! But Mozart lasts forever!

> —Ali Smith, *Autumn*

Print a famous foreskin and the world will beat a path to your door.

> —Jann Wenner, on publishing a naked photo of John Lennon in
> *Rolling Stone*

The death of God left the angels in a strange position.

> —Donald Barthelme, "On Angels"

Who needed God? We had our bodies, bread,
And glasses of a raw, green, local wine.

> —Mark Jarman, "Unholy Sonnet 13"

Did you also sacrifice a goat?

> —Daniel Dennett, to someone who said he was praying for him

If God really wanted to show off his work, he'd be a DJ.

> —Charles Taylor, *Opening Wednesday at a Theater or Drive-In near You*

It ought to make us feel ashamed when we talk like we know what we're talking about when we talk about love.

> —Raymond Carver, *Where I'm Calling From*

I barely knew I had skin before I met you.

> —Sarah Waters, *The Paying Guests*

Kiss me, and you will see how important I am.

> —Sylvia Plath, *The Unabridged Journals*

Charlene kissed convulsively, as if she had just swallowed a golf ball and was trying to force it back up.

> —Larry McMurtry, *The Last Picture Show*

They kissed as if they were sipping *crème de menthe* through a straw.

> —A. J. Liebling, quoting a friend on society women, *Between Meals*

All my life I have been hoping that someone will compare me to *crème de menthe*, which is indeed the most refreshing of drinks.

> —Auberon Waugh, *The Diaries of Auberon Waugh*

The locomotive coughed, spat, sneezed, and departed.

> —Alexandre Dumas, "Mustard"

I would like to visit the factory that makes train horns, and ask them how they are able to arrive at that chord of eternal mournfulness.

—Nicholson Baker, *A Box of Matches*

What did people have nightmares about before there were trains?

—Iris Murdoch, *Under the Net*

Live every minute as if you are late for the last train.

—Colson Whitehead, *The Colossus of New York*

People's backyards are much more interesting than their front gardens, and houses that back on to railways are public benefactors.

—John Betjeman

Henry got around.
I can't say it improved him
but unquestionably it gave him some to think about.

—John Berryman, "Dream Song 349"

We can't stop *here*. This is bat country!

—Hunter S. Thompson, *Fear and Loathing in Las Vegas*

I would rather fight a lion than be put in a roomful of bats.

—Oscar Zeta Acosta, *The Uncollected Works*

It's ill guessing what the bats are flying after.

—George Eliot, *Adam Bede*

Despair's a sweet meat I'd hang a fang in.
  —Charles Wright, "The Appalachian Book of the Dead II"

The worst [animal to eat] was a mole—that was utterly horrible.
  —Augustus J. C. Hare, *The Story of My Life*

Let things taste of what they are.
  —Alice Waters, *The Art of Simple Food*

If I see any more handcrafts I'll go mad!
  —Elizabeth Bishop, *Paris Review* interview

All forms of needlework of the fancy order are inventions of the evil one.
  —Elizabeth von Arnim, *Elizabeth and Her German Garden*

Even the swap meets around here are getting pretty corrupt.
  —Bob Dylan and Sam Shepard, "Brownsville Girl"

Few people alive at the time were more delightful, more ingenious, more movingly lovely, and, as it might happen, more savage, than the girls of slender means.
  —Muriel Spark, *The Girls of Slender Means*

I was always desired. But now I am valued. And that is a different thing, I find.
  —Hilary Mantel, *Wolf Hall*

Whatever is on the outside can be taken away at any time. Only what is inside you is safe.

—Jeanette Winterson, *Why Be Happy When You Could Be Normal?*

I was supposed to have a script, and had mislaid it. I was supposed to hear cues, and no longer did.

—Joan Didion, *The White Album*

We talked filth for a pleasant half hour.

—William Boyd, *Any Human Heart*

Expletive Delighted!

—Fairport Convention, album title

Do you appreciate that an oyster has, among its other organs, a heart?

—Padgett Powell, *The Interrogative Mood*

The best was Olivia the Oyster Dancer who would place a raw oyster on her forehead and lean back and shimmy it down all over her body without ever dropping it . . . Then she would kick it high into the air and would catch it on her forehead and begin again.

—Michael Ondaatje, *Coming Through Slaughter*

Cooling himself with an oyster.

—Charles Dickens, *Sketches by Boz*

Hang around the barbershop long enough, she said, and you'll end up with a haircut.

—Rachel Kushner, *The Mars Room*

Our hair may look stylish now,
but in the photograph it always turns against us.

—Lucia Perillo, "300D"

Charm is not a hairstyle . . . The more you try to be fashionable, the tackier you'll look.

—Ottessa Moshfegh, *My Year of Rest and Relaxation*

I read Gibbon when I curled my hair at night.

—Emily Shore, diary

Pull down thy vanity,
I say pull down.

—Erza Pound, "Canto LXXXI"

See? You set your little poosy over this spray, get the water going like this, and presto! You have a nice, clean little twattie.

—Berenice Abbott, on bidets

Dipping his ass like doughnuts in tea.

—Robert Coover, on a bidet, *Going Out for a Beer*

Luxury hotels are the real houses of God.

—Peter Cameron, *Andorra*

My hotel was not the best in town and my room was not the best in the hotel.

 —Robert Penn Warren, *All the King's Men*

There should have been a pair of signs out front, flashing back and forth: NOT QUITE A DUMP AT DUMP PRICES.

 —Charles Portis, "Motel Life, Lower Reaches"

—Do you have a reservation? she says.
—I have severe ones, he says, but I do need a room.

 —Kevin Barry, *Beatlebone*

Honk if you wish all difficult poems were profound.

 —Ben Lerner, *The Lichtenburg Figures*

It's just a poem, not a platter of brains.

 —Chelsey Minnis, "Greatness"

I'm a freak user of words, not a poet.

 —Dylan Thomas, *The Love Letters of Dylan Thomas*

It's unbelievable what they say about poetry. There must be a stable of morons somewhere kept exclusively for this purpose.

 —Howard Moss, to Elizabeth Bishop

I've had it with these cheap sons of bitches who claim they love poetry but never buy a book.

 —Kenneth Rexroth

My own prescription for making poetry popular in the schools
would be to ban it—with possession treated as a serious
misdemeanor, and dealing as a felony.

—Clive James

A codpiece that hath no poem in it is a foolish codpiece.

—Edward St. Aubyn, *Lost for Words*

When you've been made to feel bad for so long, you jump at
the chance to do it to others.

—ZZ Packer, "Brownies"

I and the public know
What all schoolchildren learn,
Those to whom evil is done
Do evil in return.

—W. H. Auden, "September 1, 1939"

All right, then I will go to hell.

—Mark Twain, *The Adventures of Huckleberry Finn*

I'm bad and I'm going to hell, and I don't care. I'd rather be in hell
than anywhere where you are.

—William Faulkner

People who die bad don't stay in the ground.

—Toni Morrison, *Beloved*

The devil's motorcycle never breaks down.

—Mischa Berlinski, *Peacekeeping*

My head is bald, my breath is bad,
Unshaven is my chin.

> —John Betjeman, "Late-Flowering Lust"

Her body's no longer tender,
but her mind is free.

> —Rita Dove, "Obedience"

Give us a touch, Poldy.

> —James Joyce, *Ulysses*

Yoda looks like a wonton and talks like a fortune cookie.

> —Pauline Kael, *For Keeps*

Totally unoriginal, feebly plotted, instantly forgettable.

> —J. G. Ballard, on *Star Wars*

The early bird who gets the worm works for somebody who comes
in late and owns the worm farm.

> —John D. MacDonald, *The Dreadful Lemon Sky*

The less important you are in an office, the more they expect the
happy smile.

> —Don DeLillo, *Libra*

We tried not to smile, for smiling only encourages men to bore you
and waste your time.

> —Sheila Heti, *How Should a Person Be?*

Do I have to stare into his eyes
and sympathize? If I want my job
I do.

　—Deborah Garrison, "Please Fire Me"

Thousands upon thousands of people who I believe are like me are those who have never found the professional skin to fit the riot in their souls.

　—Seymour Krim, *What's This Cat's Story*

Listen, here's what I'd like to do: I'd like to live in a trailer and play records all night.

　—Charles Portis, *Norwood*

My Old Kentucky Home and *Casey Jones*,
Some Sunny Day. I heard a road-gang chanting so.

　—Hart Crane, "The River"

Men and women have been living and dying for a long time, and some of them have left records.

　—Michael Robbins, *Equipment for Living*

Hail, hail rock 'n' roll
Deliver me from the days of old.

　—Chuck Berry, "School Days"

It has been said that a pretty face is a passport. But it's not, it's a visa, and it runs out fast.

　—Julie Burchill

It is the journey from ingénue to engineer, and the clock is always on.
  —Rupert Everett, *Red Carpets and Other Banana Skins*

The male version of the wax is officially called a *sunga*, which is the name for the Brazilian boys' bikini. I regret to inform you that the colloquial term for the business is "sack, back, and crack."
  —Christopher Hitchens, *And Yet*

Thank god my looks are improving, but am I getting more radical?
  —Auberon Waugh, *The Diaries of Auberon Waugh*

You have to eat eggs on the road.
  —Norman Mailer, on author tours, in *Mentor* by Tom Grimes

My life was the best omelet you could make with a chainsaw.
  —Thomas McGuane, attributed

It serves me right for putting all my eggs in one bastard.
  —Dorothy Parker

Wanda Jackson sounded like she could fry eggs on her mons veneris.
  —Nick Tosches, *Unsung Heroes of Rock 'n' Roll*

Two eggs,
over queasy.
  —Kevin Young, "Stills"

Just give me my potato, any kind of potato, and I'm happy.
  —Dolly Parton, in *The New York Times*

Words that are horrible to one writer may not be horrible to another, but if you are a writer for whom no words are terrible, you would do well to take up some other activity.

—*The Economist Style Guide*

The reader can sense whether a word is borrowed or it belongs to you.

—Michael Hofmann, *Paris Review* interview

Be suspicious of any word you learned
and were proud of learning.
It will go bad.
It will fall off the page.

—Miller Williams, "Let Me Tell You"

Should there be a breathalyzer lock on the nuclear football?
A brain scan?

—Ron Rosenbaum, *How the End Begins*

Two white guys standing next to a swimming pool full of gasoline arguing over who's got more matches.

—Stokely Carmichael, on the arms race

Them that die'll be the lucky ones.

—Robert Louis Stevenson, *Treasure Island*

You know, I'd like to have a secret lab like that myself.

—William Eggleston, on Los Alamos

If you want to say something radical, you should dress conservative.
   —Steve Biko, attributed

If people turn to look at you on the street, you are not well dressed.
   —Beau Brummell

True elegance is a real time suck, and flair misfires worse than being dull.
   —Tina Brown, *The Vanity Fair Diaries*

The average person who wears a bow tie is distrusted by almost everyone.
   —John T. Molloy

We melt into our ecstasies as though they were jams.
   —Violette Leduc, *The Lady and the Little Fox Fur*

The thin red jellies within you or within me.
   —Walt Whitman, "I Sing the Body Electric"

Ah, those knock-out body fluids: blood, sperm, tears!
   —Jean Genet, *Querelle*

What if our bodies were transparent, like a washing machine window? . . . Lovers would love more. God damn! Look at that old semen go!
   —Lucia Berlin, *A Manual for Cleaning Women*

I do give sublime blow jobs. I think I will have my mouth insured by Lloyd's of London.

    —Gael Greene, *Blue Skies, No Candy*

Everybody thinks they're good at sucking dick but they're not, usually.

    —Garth Greenwell, *Cleanness*

It really bothered him that I didn't swallow. I said to him, Are you crazy? That shit is *alive*.

    —Sigrid Nunez, *Naked Sleeper*

Trying out the bad banana taste of Durex on your tongue.

    —Hannah Sullivan, "You, Very Young in New York"

When you spend many hours alone in a room
you have more than the usual chances to disgust yourself

    —Lucia Perillo, "Again, the Body"

Let's hate each other with our minds, not our bodies!

    —Chelsey Minnis, "Depression"

It is a rule of Shakespeare production that men who eat grapes are definitely voluptuaries and probably murderers.

    —Kenneth Tynan, *Right and Left*

Lord, let me eat more fruit
than comes in a mixed drink.

    —Kevin Young, "Sleepwalking Psalms"

I pick twenty [cherries] at a time and stuff them all into my mouth
at once. They taste better like that.

—Anton Chekhov, *A Life in Letters*

I don't think I ever had a cherry. If I did, it got shoved so far back I
was usin' it for a tail-light.

—Dolly Parton, in *Rolling Stone*

What peaches and what penumbras! Whole families shopping
   at night!
Aisles full of husbands!

—Allen Ginsberg, "A Supermarket in California"

Here we go round the prickly pear
Prickly pear prickly pear
Here we go round the prickly pear
At five o'clock in the morning.

—T. S. Eliot, "The Hollow Men"

Debauchee of dew.

—Emily Dickinson

[He] would rather fuck a prominent girl than a pretty one.

—Wolcott Gibbs, on a *New Yorker* colleague

Civilisation meant good company and going to bed with anyone you
liked.

—Kenneth Clark's synopsis of Clive Bell's *Civilisation*

What I am saying, Doctor, is that I don't seem to stick my dick up these girls, as much as I stick it up their backgrounds—as though through fucking I will discover America.

—Philip Roth, *Portnoy's Complaint*

Real artists are not nice people; all their best feelings go into their work, and life has the residue.

—W. H. Auden

Don't confuse the monster on the page with the monster here in front of you.

—Donald Barthelme

A monster is a person who has stopped pretending.

—Colson Whitehead, "A Psychotronic Childhood"

It's not nice; it's art.

—Bertolt Brecht

I had seen enough of fashionable society to know that it is there that one finds real illiteracy and not, let us say, among electricians.

—Marcel Proust, *In Search of Lost Time*

I think that a garbage collector is as sensitive as any author.

—J. P. Donleavy, *Paris Review* interview

I . . . would have daily taken out her garbage just to be near her can.

—Chuck Berry, *The Autobiography*

When we championed trash culture, we had no idea it would become the only culture.

—Pauline Kael

I published it in my W.P.B.

—Rudyard Kipling, *The Letters of Rudyard Kipling, 1920–1930*

If I can't walk, I can't write.

—Sigrid Nunez, *The Friend*

I have come from Alabama: a fur piece. All the way from Alabama a-walking. A fur piece.

—William Faulkner, *Light in August*

This walking business is overrated. I mastered the art of doing it when I was quite small, and in any case, what are taxis for?

—Christopher Hitchens, *And Yet*

Bruce Chatwin liked to hike naked with flowers tied around his penis.

—A fact reported in Bruce Chatwin, *Under the Sun*

The flowers you gave me—they died.

—Patricia Highsmith, *The Price of Salt*

Thunder is my favorite color.

—Frederick Seidel, "Envoi"

The 4 a.m. Show.

—Les Murray, on his demons, *Killing the Black Dog*

It's always night, or we wouldn't need light.

  —Thelonious Monk

The light at the end of the tunnel is just the light of an oncoming train.

  —Robert Lowell

If you don't know the exact moment the lights will go out, you might as well read until they do.

  —Clive James, *Latest Readings*

Optimism? What is that?

  —Voltaire, *Candide*

I'm the first person who'll put it to you and the last person who'll explain it to you.

  —Bob Dylan, *Rolling Stone* interview

He's just another man who wants to teach me something.

  —Sheila Heti, *How Should a Person Be?*

This was the usual thing. What I asked for was facts: what I got was a sermon.

  —Hilary Mantel, *An Experiment in Love*

Men explain things to me, still. And no man has ever apologized for explaining, wrongly, things that I know and they don't.

  —Rebecca Solnit, *Men Explain Things to Me*

He was a village explainer, excellent if you were a village, but if not, not.

  —Gertrude Stein, on Ezra Pound

I took a little celebrational nap.

—Renata Adler, *Speedboat*

Don't forget daily and fully undressed naps.

—Jim Harrison, *The Raw and the Cooked*

I want to sleep in her uterus with my foot hanging out.

—Barry Hannah, "Love Too Long"

A nap ending precisely at sunset, with its undead overtones, was rarely a good idea.

—Jonathan Lethem, *A Gambler's Anatomy*

Sleep is the most moronic fraternity in the world.

—Vladimir Nabokov, *Speak, Memory*

Sleep only means red-cheeks and red-cheeks are not the fit adornments of Caesar.

—Wallace Stevens, *Letters of Wallace Stevens*

Somatize and the living is easy.

—Ali Smith, *Spring*

I'd love to fuck your wife.

—Harry Crews, to Tom McGuane

Musical beds is the faculty sport around here.

—Edward Albee, *Who's Afraid of Virginia Woolf?*

Oh, the heartbreak of satyriasis.
> —Fran Ross, *Oreo*

There's no loathing like self-loathing.
> —Barbara Hamby, "Hatred"

The only thing lower than me was a dead man.
> —Richard Brautigan, *Dreaming of Babylon*

My self-esteem is so low that getting the Pulitzer Prize just made me break even.
> —Franz Wright

Root tee toot, ahhh root tee toot, oh we're the members of the Institute.
> —John Cheever, when elected to the National Institute of Arts and Letters

America takes her writers too seriously.
> —Kingsley Amis

Don't fuck the contributors.
> —Harold Ross

I'll show you something that isn't in the Tate.
> —Tate Museum Director James Bolivar Manson, leeringly

I don't want a restaurant where a jazz band can't come marching through.
> —Ella Brennan, of Commander's Palace

If Emily Dickinson owned a restaurant it would be Chez Panisse.

—Jason Epstein, *Eating: A Memoir*

The great unrecognized merit of *haute cuisine* is that it makes you drunk.

—Kenneth Tynan, *Right and Left*

Like the heavy judgment of God on the sinner, the bill came.

—Robert Hughes, *The Spectacle of Skill*

The Laughing Room.

—Damon Runyon, on where he imagined the owners of the '21' Club gathered to set menu prices

That was some weird shit.

—George W. Bush, on Donald Trump's inauguration speech

How much of this nonsense does he believe, I wonder, and how much does he say just because he knows the value of dividing in order to conquer and to rule?

—Octavia E. Butler, *Parable of the Talents*

[I am] thankful that I am old and have no children to leave in a world at the mercy of this lying and bellicose vulgarian.

—Alan Bennett, on Donald Trump, in *London Review of Books*

He's the weasel in the tube jammed up our asses.

—Nell Zink, *Doxology*

The one good thing about national anthems is that we're already on our feet, and therefore ready to run.

> —Ocean Vuong, *On Earth We're Briefly Gorgeous*

The Declaration [of Independence] is like a map. You trust that it's right, but you only know by going out and testing it yourself.

> —Colson Whitehead, *The Underground Railroad*

Help us to make America great again.

> —Octavia E. Butler, *Parable of the Talents*

Your Flag Decal Won't Get You into Heaven Anymore.

> —John Prine, song title

—What is the worst thing anyone's said to you?
—Your first line contains a dangler.

> —Ian McEwan, *Guardian* interview

Typos are worse than fascism.

> —I. F. Stone

When I split an infinitive, God damn it, I split it so it will stay split.

> —Raymond Chandler, *Selected Letters*

You put down what you want to say. Then you get somebody to add in the commas and shit where they belong.

> —Elmore Leonard, *Get Shorty*

Substitute "damn" every time you're inclined to write "very"; your editor will delete it and the writing will be just as it should be.

> —Mark Twain, *Notebooks*

I am writing the Great American Suicide Note.

—Bob Kaufman, "Bonsai Poems"

Kill me, por favor.

—Ry Cooder, short story title

What can I do for you except give you directions to the Golden Gate Bridge and a few basics on how to jump?

—Richard Brautigan, *Dreaming of Babylon*

Didn't Robert Lowell say, if people were equipped with switches, who wouldn't be tempted, at some point, to flick themselves off?

—Lucia Perillo, "Daisies vs. Bees"

Jesus, Jesus, Jesus. Help me. Please, help me. If you really exist, you skinny jew bastard, help me kill myself.

—Hubert Selby, Jr., *Waiting Period*

Lay my head on the railroad line, Train come along, pacify my mind.

—Toni Morrison, *Beloved*

Suicide is, after all, the opposite of the poem.

—Anne Sexton

Shrink it and pink it.

—Designers, traditionally, on products for women

You've got to make yourself more cupcakeable.

—Helen Gurley Brown

It is sometimes, as a feminist in the world, difficult to stay pleased.

—Lorrie Moore, *See What Can Be Done*

Pretty good, for a woman.

—William Faulkner, on Evelyn Scott

Beware of the man who denounces woman writers; his penis is tiny & cannot spell.

—Erica Jong, "Seventeen Warnings in Search of a Feminist Poem"

A good part—and definitely the most fun part—of being a feminist is about frightening men.

—Julie Burchill

Bryn Mawr had done what a four-year dose of liberal education was designed to do: unfit her for eighty percent of the useful work of the world.

—Toni Morrison, *Song of Solomon*

My PhD advisor told me to put a ten dollar bill between the pages of my thesis in the university library. So I can check to see if anyone read it? I asked. No, of course no one will read it, he replied, but when you come back into town you'll always have money for lunch.

—Carl T. Bergstrom, on Twitter

The only purpose of a university education is to teach people to enjoy life more than they would have done otherwise.
>   —Auberon Waugh, *The Diaries of Auberon Waugh*

You can get straight A's and still flunk life.
>   —Walker Percy, *The Second Coming*

I tell you I can't read a book, but I can read de people.
>   —Sojourner Truth

When body odour and volubility meet, there is no remedy.
>   —Samuel Beckett, *Murphy*

Every stink that fights the ventilator thinks it is Don Quixote.
>   —Stanislaw Lem

All it comes down to is this: I feel like shit but look great.
>   —Bret Easton Ellis, *American Psycho*

My schedule for today lists a six-hour self-accusatory depression.
>   —Philip K. Dick, *Do Androids Dream of Electric Sheep?*

—Doesn't a day like this make you glad to be alive?
—I wouldn't go as far as that.
>   —Samuel Beckett

One reason the human race has such a low opinion of itself is that it gets so much of its wisdom from writers.
>   —Wilfrid Sheed, *The Good Word and Other Words*

With this incredible illness *everything* sucks. The glorious dawn
sucks. The *Coronation Mass* sucks!

—William Styron, on depression, from an unfinished novel

We all had depression, but Bill was the only one who made money
out of it.

—Art Buchwald, on William Styron

Tell Bill Styron to deal with this!

—Stanley Elkin, on using a wheelchair because of his multiple sclerosis

The tornadoed Atlantic of my being.

—Herman Melville, *Moby-Dick*

I was Pearl Harbor'd. December Seventh'd by the Lord.

—Stanley Elkin, *The Living End*

I can't stand THE DEPRESSED. It's like a job, it's the only thing they
work hard at.

—Deborah Levy, *Swimming Home*

A contact low.

—Jonathan Franzen, *Freedom*

I believe in white supremacy.

—John Wayne, *Playboy* interview, 1971

If somebody told me I had only one hour to live, I'd spend it
choking a white man. I'd do it nice and slow.

—Miles Davis

Unbelievably, Miles Davis & John Coltrane
Standing within inches of each other didn't explode.

> —Terrance Hayes, *American Sonnets for My Past and Future Assassin*

The musical embodiment of a lonely-hearts ad with carefully
phrased undertones of sex.

> —Kenneth Tynan, on Miles Davis, *Tynan Right and Left*

Play that.

> —Miles Davis, to his band, pointing toward a woman who'd
> stumbled in the street

Thelonious Monk, are you still bopping
someplace down below?

> —Stephen Dobyns, "Lullaby"

Remember literature, Charlie? It involved getting drunk and
getting laid.

> —Don DeLillo, *Mao II*

What's the novel about if not getting fucked.

> —Olivia Laing, *Crudo*

I was home writing. I stopped going out . . . I didn't fuck anyone new.

> —Eve Babitz, *Eve's Hollywood*

What will fatten you, skinny little book?

> —Karl Shapiro, *The Bourgeois Poet*

I preferred my prose with extra wontons.

—Robert Christgau, *Going into the City*

[Cyril] Connolly famously marked his place in a book he had borrowed with a rasher of bacon.

—Mary-Kay Wilmers, *Human Relations and Other Difficulties*

Write a novel . . . A short one, they sell much better.

—Iris Murdoch, *Living on Paper*

If we don't show anyone, we're free to write anything.

—Allen Ginsberg, *Cosmopolitan Greetings*

—You mean, you made it all up, and they taken it and give you real money for it?
—Yes, Ma. Yes, they have.

—Harry Crews and his mother, Myrtice, after he sold his first novel

Sometimes life is merely a matter of coffee and whatever intimacy a cup of coffee affords.

—Richard Brautigan, *Revenge of the Lawn*

Then . . . there is that liquid the English call coffee.

—Virginia Woolf, *To the Lighthouse*

If this is coffee, please bring me some tea, but if this is tea, please bring me some coffee.

—Abraham Lincoln, attributed

Coffee's for closers only.

—David Mamet, *Glengarry Glen Ross*

Fresh newsprint, good coffee, assorted texts, some messages on her BlackBerry, what more could the modern world offer?

    —Margaret Drabble, *The Dark Flood Rises*

Whenever he walked into the dining-room, I raised my glass and smashed it on the table, as every gentleman does in the presence of homosexuals.

    —Ernest Hemingway

They tell me that Mr. Hemingway usually kicks people like me in the crotch.

    —Tennessee Williams

Let's face it, sweetheart—without Jews, fags, and gypsies, there is no theater.

    —Mel Brooks, in *To Be or Not to Be*

There are three kinds of pianists: Jewish pianists, homosexual pianists, and bad pianists.

    —Vladimir Horowitz

I don't know where you'd find such a magazine.

    —Kenneth Koch, attributed, on a stipulation that the staff of *The Harvard Advocate* contain no Jews, homosexuals, or drunks

If you removed all of the homosexuals and homosexual influence from what is generally regarded as American culture you would be pretty much left with *Let's Make a Deal*.

    —Fran Lebowitz, in *The New York Times*

What is it about being on a boat that makes everyone behave like a film star?

—Evelyn Waugh, *Brideshead Revisited*

A luxury liner is really just a bad play surrounded by water.

—Clive James

If you don't like my story get out of the punt.

—James Joyce, *Finnegans Wake*

We are a paper frigate sailing on a burning lake.

—Frederick Seidel, "France Now"

Now it's my turn for the boat with the hole in it.

—Ali Smith, *Spring*

Old and young, we are all on our last cruise.

—Robert Louis Stevenson, "Crabbed Age and Youth"

One is very vulnerable in a deck chair.

—Iris Murdoch, *The Black Prince*

Today's smugglers are just your deck-chair dozers.

—Joseph McElroy, *A Smuggler's Bible*

We had gone back and forth all night on the ferry.

—Edna St. Vincent Millay, "Recuerdo"

Few things hold the perceptions more thoroughly captive than anxiety about what we have got to say.

—George Eliot

If you can give a decent speech in public or cut any kind of figure on the podium, then you never need dine or sleep alone.

—Christopher Hitchens, *Hitch-22*

[He] should not be delivering a State of the Union address. He should be delivering pizza.

—Clive James, on George W. Bush

Don't own anything you wouldn't leave out in the rain.

—Gary Snyder

I'd rather have roses on my table than diamonds around my neck.

—Emma Goldman, attributed

I saw the best minds of my generation destroyed by payment plans.

—Kate Tempest, "Sigh"

Buttered toast with cunty fingers.

—The best breakfast, according to Henry Green, *Paris Review* interview

I do like a little bit of butter to my bread!

—A. A. Milne, "The King's Breakfast"

Du beurre! Donnez-moi du beurre! Toujours du beurre!

—Fernand Point

By what inevitable degrees does bent become inclination, inclination tendency, tendency penchant, penchant disposition, disposition fate?

—Stanley Elkin, *The Dick Gibson Show*

Fate was working its ass off when it got us all together.

—Elmore Leonard, attributed

You couldn't find your ass with both hands.

—Saul Bellow, *Humboldt's Gift*

It is good for a man to eat thistles, and to remember that he is an ass.

—E. S. Dallas, on artichokes, *Kettner's Book of the Table*

All I want to do is sit on my ass and fart and think of Dante.

—Samuel Beckett

People don't look up to you as a hero when you tell them you were shot in the ass.

—Richard Brautigan, *Dreaming of Babylon*

Read at whim! Read at whim!

—Randall Jarrell

Death to all modifiers.

—Joseph Heller, *Catch-22*

When we ask for advice, we are usually asking for an accomplice.

—Saul Bellow, attributed

Everybody who tells you how to act has whisky on their breath.

—John Updike, *Rabbit, Run*

High-Tech Redneck.

—George Jones, song title

Dickheads from Dixie.

> —What Cy Twombly said a group memoir of himself, Robert
> Rauschenberg, and Jasper Johns would be called

I twang it out and leave it there.

> —Wallace Stevens, "The Man with the Blue Guitar"

They twanged each other's underpants.

> —Kevin Barry, *Night Boat to Tangier*

She gets the gravity of the floppy dick just right.

> —David Salle, on a painting by Dana Schutz, in *Artforum*

You have to talk to these art world assholes like you give even
less of a fuck than they do.

> —Greg Jackson, *Prodigals*

Nobody owns life, but anyone who can pick up a frying pan
owns death.

> —William S. Burroughs

One minute in a skull and the next in a belly.

> —Samuel Beckett, *The Unnamable*

No matter what you do, someone always gets boiled.

> —Margaret Atwood, on fairy tales, *The Robber Bride*

We boil at different degrees.

> —Ralph Waldo Emerson, "Eloquence"

You saw my book? What was it doing?

   —Dan Jenkins, *His Ownself*

Where's jazz going? I don't know where it's going. Maybe it's going to hell.

   —Thelonious Monk

Fuck the general reader, Solly said, because in fact the general reader doesn't exist. That's what I say, Edwina yelled. Just fuck the general reader.

   —Muriel Spark, *Loitering with Intent*

Well, fuck the plot! That is for precocious schoolboys. What matters is the imaginative truth.

   —Edna O'Brien, *Paris Review* interview

It is the easiest thing in the world for a man to look as if he had a great secret in him.

   —Herman Melville, *Moby-Dick*

I will take his secret to the grave, telling people I meet on the way.

   —Tom Stoppard, *The Invention of Love*

Shut up, he explained.

   —Ring Lardner, *The Young Immigrunts*

Merry Christmas! the man threatened.

   —William Gaddis, *The Recognitions*

Alacrity she served.

    —James Joyce, *Ulysses*

Imagine having a very small dick—how vast and unknowable the universe must be to the small-dicked man!

    —Sheila Heti, *Motherhood*

Bob [Geldof] had a cock so big he needed a wheelbarrow to carry it around in . . . Everything about him announced the fact: the incredibly thin body, the large pushy nose, the jungle smell of the man.

    —Rupert Everett, *Red Carpets and Other Banana Skins*

He didn't need pants, he needed Parking Privileges.

    —Allan Gurganus, in *Interview* magazine

He got that Jesus with a hard dick complex.

    —Tish Benson, "Fifth-Ward E-mail"

A feller can get along with false teeth and a glass eye and hearing aids and even a hook or a wooden leg if he has to, but there ain't no known substitute for a big dick.

    —Larry McMurtry, *The Last Picture Show*

Yo daddy walk like a broke dick dog.

    —Hattie Gossett, "yo daddy: an 80s version of the dozens"

Gary's Got a Boner.

    —The Replacements, song title

If a sentence is wordy, then it's never witty.

—Clive James, *Latest Readings*

Good things, when short, are twice as good.

—Tom Stoppard, attributed

Vive la bagatelle!

—Jonathan Swift

It was so droll it was practically retarded.

—Joy Williams, "The Girls"

Take eloquence and wring its neck.

—Paul Verlaine

I can write better than anybody who can write faster, and I can write faster than anybody who can write better.

—A. J. Liebling

I call that bold talk for a one-eyed fat man.

—Charles Portis, *True Grit*

People will say anything to appear interesting.

—Olivia Manning, *Fortunes of War*

You're a disgrace to your clip-on tie.

—David Mitchell, *Slade House*

I'd rather talk about other people. Gossip, or as we gossips like to say, character analysis.

—Elizabeth Hardwick, *Paris Review* interview

There are few things harder to imagine than other people's conversations about yourself.

—Jonathan Franzen, *Freedom*

There is nothing more provocative than minding your own business.

—William S. Burroughs, *The Place of Dead Roads*

As a husband you are . . . PUNK!!

—Dolly Grey to Zane Grey

[I've had] more meaningful relationships with people I've sat next to on aeroplanes.

—Angela Carter, on her first husband

If you can hoe corn for fifty cents an hour, day after day, you can learn how to write a novel.

—Jim Harrison, *Paris Review* interview

You don't have to be an intellectual to write, you just have to wonder about things and want to know.

—Barry Hannah, *Paris Review* interview

I knew the alphabet. Maybe I could be a writer.

—Hubert Selby, Jr.

I figured writing would be like learning how to build houses or lay brick . . . If I wrote long enough and hard enough, I'd eventually learn how.

—Larry Brown, *On Fire*

Thackeray had to pay to publish *Vanity Fair*. Sterne had to pay to publish *Tristram Shandy*. Defoe had to pay to publish *Moll Flanders*.

    —David Markson, *Reader's Block*

The writer of novels has found the oil and anointed himself.

    —Saul Bellow, "Distractions of a Fiction Writer"

A writer who doesn't keep up with what's out there ain't gonna be out there.

    —Toni Cade Bambara

Organdie and seersucker are pretty thin materials.

    —Robert Penn Warren, on the sexiness of summer dancing,
      All the King's Men

I could not reveal my findings over the public-address system at the dance.

    —Terry Southern, "Twirling at Ole Miss"

Swing! your partner, promenade (and when you can get laid get laid).

    —A. R. Ammons, *Tape for the Turn of the Year*

Sissy Spacek with a wicked case of intestinal flu.

    —Spalding Grey, on a mental image to delay orgasm, *The Journals*
      of Spalding Grey

Winston Churchill.

    —The name the young John Lennon would call out while others
      were saying names like "Brigitte Bardot," to ruin lights-out
      masturbation sessions

Oh! Nnnnnnn! Nnn! Nnn! Nnn! Nnn! Nnn! Nnn!

    —Nicholson Baker, *Vox*

My father lost me to the Beast at cards.

    —First sentence of Angela Carter's "The Tiger's Bride"

Someone cut the cards wrong at the beginning, and it's been like that all along.

    —Ian Fleming, letter

Here was the crux of my dilemma: I felt like killing my father, but I didn't want him to die.

    —Ottessa Moshfegh, *Eileen*

I basically want nothing to do with all men except my son, my father, and a few others.

    —Nicholson Baker, *A Box of Matches*

I didn't want to see anything worse than me befall her.

    —Larry Brown, *Big Bad Love*

Obsessions are the only things that matter.

    —Patricia Highsmith, diary

I don't know if you're a detective or a pervert.

    —Laura Dern, to Kyle MacLachlan, in *Blue Velvet*

I love my work with a love that is frantic and perverted, as an ascetic loves the hair shirt that scratches his belly.

    —Gustave Flaubert, *The Letters of Gustave Flaubert: 1830–1857*

Perversion is better than no version at all.

—A. R. Ammons, "The Prescriptive Stalls As"

Even ordinary objects, such as table-tennis paddles, can be adapted as "good pervertables."

—Camille Paglia, on S&M, "Scholars in Bondage"

A university is just a group of buildings gathered around a library.

—Shelby Foote

My alma mater is the Chicago Public Library.

—David Mamet

You see, books had been happening to me.

—Langston Hughes, *The Big Sea*

Three call slips at a time.

—Ta-Nehisi Coates, *Between the World and Me*

Leave this bar. Walk west on Forty-second till you come to Fifth. You'll see two great stone lions. Walk up the steps between those two lions, get yourself a library card and don't be an idiot.

—Frank McCourt, *Tis*

I see you have written a book about yourself and called it *The World Crisis*.

—Arthur Balfour, to Winston Churchill

When you're buying books, you're optimistically thinking you're buying the time to read them.

—Arthur Schopenhauer

I'm not going to die, I'm going home like a shooting star.
    —Sojourner Truth

The heaventree of stars hung with humid nightblue fruit.
    —James Joyce, *Ulysses*

Beneath those stars is a universe of gliding monsters.
    —Herman Melville

There is nothing more alone than being in a car at night in the rain.
    —Robert Penn Warren, *All the King's Men*

If you want to commune with the dead, of course what you have to do is drive across the night to Missouri.
    —Peter Orner, *Maggie Brown and Others*

Girls in Rolls-Royces, their faces lit by the dash.
    —James Salter, *Light Years*

It's imperative to have a place to base for face to face.
    —Chuck Berry, on cars, *The Autobiography*

When it gets dark I tow your heart away.
    —The Beatles, "Lovely Rita"

Our mothers always remain the strangest, craziest people we've ever met.
    —Marguerite Duras, *Practicalities*

My mother beat me in 4/4 time.

 —Sharon Olds, "Silver Spoon Ode"

He had a mother who was less a mother than a gypsy curse.

 —Roberto Bolaño, *Between Parentheses*

Mother, I want the birthday supper of my childhood,
dripping with sauce.

 —Rita Dove, "Lullaby"

Your mother asks
To be your friend again, but the request just hangs in the sidebar.

 —Hannah Sullivan, "You, Very Young in New York"

Nobody loves me but my mother—
And she could be jivin', too.

 —B.B. King, "Nobody Loves Me but My Mother"

That's my mom. I came out her asshole and I love her very much.

 —Ocean Vuong, *On Earth We're Briefly Gorgeous*

Aye Oedipus, yir a complex fucker right enough.

 —Irvine Welsh, *The Acid House*

I look eight years older than everybody.

 —Stanley Elkin, in *The New York Times*

I look dead
for my age.

 —Kevin Young, "The Escape"

Old age is always fifteen years older than I am.
>   —Bernard Baruch

It is a fact of life that people give dinner parties, and when they invite you, you have to turn around and invite them back . . . Back and forth you go, like Ping-Pong balls, and what you end up with is called social life.
>   —Laurie Colwin, *Home Cooking*

We feed others so they won't eat us.
>   —Jason Epstein, quoting a chef, *Eating: A Memoir*

While I'm slicing salami I think how much blood there is in a person's body. If you put too much stuff in things, they break.
>   —Elena Ferrante, *The Story of a New Name*

There's so much goop inside of us, man, he said, and it all wants to get out.
>   —Denis Johnson, *Jesus' Son*

Same old sausage, fizzing and sputtering in his own grease.
>   —Henry James, on Thomas Carlyle

I lit my fire, I greased my skillet, and I cooked.
>   —Charlie Parker

Go, and speed.
>   —Chaos, to Satan, in John Milton's *Paradise Lost*

I gave him a generous tip for driving so dangerously.

—Deborah Levy, *Things I Don't Want to Know*

I'll tip you just twice as much if you drive me just half as fast.

—William Shawn, to a cabdriver

A quiet smoke in
a taxi is my idea of bliss.

—James Schuyler, "A Few Days"

Is it possible that he is the late Adolf Hitler, kept alive by Count
Dracula?

—John Updike, on a cabdriver, *Bech: A Book*

She decided he was a vampire, which added a dreamlike, sinister
undertone to his chattiness.

—Kate Christensen, on a cabdriver, *The Last Cruise*

I watched her leave for the airport, and said to myself that nothing
resembled an ambulance more than a taxicab.

—Philippe Lançon, *Disturbance*

In my experience the spider is the smallest creature whose gaze
can be felt.

—Iris Murdoch, *Under the Net*

You are no a de wrider, you are de espider, and we shoota de
espiders in Mejico.

—Malcolm Lowry, *Under the Volcano*

Will you walk into my wavetrap? said the spiter to the shy.
    —James Joyce, *Finnegans Wake*

The crow mocks the ant's short life from afar.
    —Adam Clay, "Understories"

The ants are my friends, they're blowing in the wind.
    —Lorrie Moore, *Anagrams*

The easiest way for your child to learn about money is for you not
to have any.
    —Katharine Whitehorn

Real wealth is never having to spend time with assholes.
    —John Waters

Money won't change you, but time will take you on.
    —James Brown, "Money Won't Change You"

Elvis kicked "How Much is that Doggie in the Window" out the
window and replaced it with "Let's Fuck."
    —Lester Bangs, in *The Village Voice*

If Elvis Presley is
King
Who is James Brown?
God?
    —Amiri Baraka, "In the Funk World"

Elvis may have been the king of rock 'n' roll, but I am the queen.
 —Little Richard

Few people know what fish think about injustice.
 —Ursula K. Le Guin, *Catwings*

Fish cannot carry guns.
 —Philip K. Dick, *Valis*

Do fish ever get seasick?
 —James Joyce, *Ulysses*

In man or fish, wriggling is a sign of inferiority.
 —Herman Melville

Being an old maid is like death by drowning, a really delightful
sensation after you cease to struggle.
 —Edna Ferber

Fish die belly-upward and rise to the surface; it is their way
of falling.
 —André Gide, *Journals: 1928–1939*

They came ashore with erections.
 —John Berryman, "The Armada Song"

The only thing I could think of was turkey neck and turkey gizzards
and I felt very depressed.
 —Esther Greenwood, on seeing her first penis, in Sylvia Plath's
 The Bell Jar

Thundertube . . . Seedstick . . . Malcolm Gladwell.
> —New names for the penis, in Nicholson Baker's *House of Holes*

He thrust his enormous Rehnquist deep within her Whizzer White.
> —Gore Vidal, *Myron*

The Old Testament contains twenty-six laughs.
> —Paul Johnson, *Humorists*

I can walk! I can walk!
> —Malcolm McDowell, running wildly down a hill at Lourdes

The best thing about being God would be making the heads.
> —Iris Murdoch, *A Severed Head*

Weeks passed, but my Word-A-Day Calendar was stuck on "motherfucker."
> —Colson Whitehead, *The Noble Hustle*

That's my bag. I'm a motherfucker.
> —Grace Paley, *Enormous Changes at the Last Minute*

And even after all my logic and my theory
I add a "Motherfucker" so you ignorant niggas hear me.
> —Fugees, "Zealots"

Desire don't *discriminate*, said Avery. Desire's gonna swallow every motherfucker out here.
> —Bryan Washington, *Lot*

The white cracker who wrote the national anthem knew what he was doing. He set the word "free" to a note so high nobody can reach it . . . I'll show you America. Terminal, crazy and mean.

—Tony Kushner, *Angels in America*

So much depends upon a red pickup truck, filled with crackers.

—Colson Whitehead, *John Henry Days*

Southern Hospitiboo.

—Chuck Berry's term for politeness mixed with hostility,
The Autobiography

I sing to thee of Shine
the stoker who was hip enough to flee the fucking ship
and let the white folks drown.

—Etheridge Knight, "Dark Prophecy: I Sing of Shine"

Being over seventy is like being engaged in a war. All our friends are going or gone and we survive amongst the dead and dying as on a battlefield.

—Muriel Spark, *Memento Mori*

Old age isn't a battle: old age is a massacre.

—Philip Roth, *Everyman*

The years between fifty and seventy are the hardest. You are always being asked to do more, and yet you are not decrepit enough to turn them down.

—T. S. Eliot, in *Time* magazine

I must go home periodically to renew my sense of horror.

—Carson McCullers

Home is where your ass is.

—William S. Burroughs, *The Wild Boys*

They all said the way to a man's heart is through his asshole.

—Edmund White, *Our Young Man*

Whoever said the soul and the body meet in the pineal gland was a fool. It's the asshole, stupid.

—André Aciman, *Call Me by Your Name*

In the ass is how you create loyalty.

—Philip Roth, *The Human Stain*

If I fucked you in the ass I would own you, he'd said.

—Mary Gaitskill, *Because They Wanted To*

Where but in the very asshole of comedown is redemption?

—A. R. Ammons, *Garbage*

The hiatus in Phutatorius's breeches was sufficiently wide to receive the chesnut.

—Laurence Sterne, *Tristram Shandy*

Words don't have ass cheeks!

—Jonathan Miles, *Dear American Airlines*

Why do born-again people so often make you wish they'd never been born the first time?

    —Katharine Whitehorn

If you gave [Jerry] Falwell an enema he'd be buried in a matchbox.

    —Christopher Hitchens, on *Hannity & Colmes*

I have no enamamies.

    —Stanley Elkin, *The Dick Gibson Show*

That's the world out there, little green apples and infectious disease.

    —Don DeLillo, *The Angel Esmeralda*

It glistened in a billion pairs of eyes.

    —Robert Stone, *A Flag for Sunrise*

All is infection, mother . . .
We shall sit quietly in this room,
and I think we'll be spared.

    —Rita Dove, "Fiammetta Breaks Her Face"

An apple a day, if well aimed, keeps the doctor away.

    —P. G. Wodehouse

Most people, inside are filled with *unexamined junk.*

    —Iris Murdoch, *Living on Paper*

It's tired and stiff and full of crud. It's a typical American heart.

    —John Updike, *Rabbit at Rest*

Some joker has made a plastic heart. Anything is possible.

—Chester Himes, *Blind Man with a Pistol*

My heart's some kind of idiotic fishing bobber.

—George Saunders, *CivilWarLand in Bad Decline*

I'm the shy heart with the side part.

—Amit Majmudar, *Dothead*

What grape, to keep its place in the sun, taught our ancestors to make wine?

—Cyril Connolly, *The Unquiet Grave*

What god leant down and whispered in what mortal ear to put walnuts inside an eggplant?

—Annia Ciezadlo, *Day of Honey*

I surveyed this dish of food and surreptitiously undid the top three buttons of my shorts.

—Gerald Durrell, *Birds, Beasts, and Relatives*

People in California live in a world of rumors, dreams, and superstitions, because newspapers out there don't print much news.

—Harold Ross, *Letters from the Editor*

It's a scientific fact that if you stay in California you lose one point of your IQ every year.

—Truman Capote

For an easterner there is never any salt in the wind; it is like Mexican cooking without chile, or Chinese egg rolls missing their mustard.

> —Norman Mailer, on Los Angeles, "Superman Comes to the Supermarket"

Too Dumb for New York City, Too Ugly for L.A.

> —Waylon Jennings, album title

Come to California. Come to these canyons if you want to be driven by sacredness into the air. If you dream of the true, clear silences to sing—come to California.

> —Denis Johnson, *Already Dead*

Let me be Los Angeles.

> —James Joyce, *Finnegans Wake*

I want more money I want more money I want more money I want more money I want more money I want more money I want more money I want more money I want more money I want more money I want more money.

> —Start of a letter from John O'Hara to Harold Ross

I used my grant to fix my teeth.

> —Ron Silliman, "Albany"

A large body of money completely surrounded by people who want some.

> —Dwight Macdonald, on the Ford Foundation

E. E. Cummings was as hot against materialist society as only a
poet living on a trust fund can be.

> —Clive James, *Poetry Notebook*

What's all the shooting for?
You have money and I haven't.

> —Chelsey Minnis, "Love"

If artists could save a man from a lifetime of digging coal by
digging it themselves one hour a week, most would refuse. Some
would commit suicide. "It's not the time, it's the anticipation! It
ruins the whole week! I can't read, much less write!"

> —Elizabeth Hardwick, *The Collected Essays of Elizabeth Hardwick*

The least pain in our little finger gives us more concern and
uneasiness, than the destruction of millions of our fellow-beings.

> —William Hazlitt

What I feel bad about is that I don't feel worse.

> —Michael Frayn

Onan.

> —Name of Dorothy Parker's canary, because it spilled its seed
>   on the ground

One inalienable right binds all mankind together—the right of
self-abuse.

> —Kenneth Tynan, *The Sound of Two Hands Clapping*

Massacre is obscene. Torture is obscene. Three million dead is obscene. Masturbation, even with an admittedly nonconsensual squid? Not so much.

—Viet Thanh Nguyen, *The Sympathizer*

The right hand = the hand that is aggressive, the hand that masturbates. Therefore, to prefer the left hand! . . . To romanticize it, to sentimentalize it!

—Susan Sontag, *As Consciousness Is Harnessed to Flesh*

I was sneaking time with my own body.

—Patricia Smith, "What You Pray Toward"

Such writing is a sort of mental masturbation—he is always f[ri]gg[in]g his *Imagination*.

—Lord Byron, on John Keats

No one who likes Yeats is capable of human intimacy.

—Sally Rooney, *Conversations with Friends*

The birds sang *tutti*, all of them.

—Delmore Schwartz, "A Small Score"

Without birds I'm dead.

—Jim Harrison, *Dead Man's Float*

Birds, except when broiled and in the society of a cold bottle, bored him stiff.

—P. G. Wodehouse, *My Man Jeeves*

Goose swoops down and plucks you out.

—Ken Kesey, *One Flew Over the Cuckoo's Nest*

Walking with the King.

—Oscar Zeta Acosta, on being on LSD

Don't worry, if we run out of drugs, we can all suck on Hunter.

—David Felton, to Timothy Crouse, in Joe Hagan's *Sticky Fingers*

Unwanted sex on acid is a nightmare.

—Mary Gaitskill, *Somebody with a Little Hammer*

Whenever a friend succeeds, a little something in me dies.

—Gore Vidal

Do your friends shun you? Do people cross the street when they see you approaching?

—Flann O'Brien, *The Best of Myles*

Gentle reader, did you ever feel yourself snubbed?

—Anthony Trollope, *The Warden*

There is no disappointment so numbing . . . as someone no better than you achieving more.

—Joseph Heller, *Good as Gold*

I spend so much time in your shadow I'm starting to get a vitamin deficiency.

—Rachel Cusk, *Transit*

Dilated to Meet You.
>   —Loudon Wainwright III, song title

Here's a tip for new parents: Start lowering those expectations early, it's going to pay off later.
>   —Colson Whitehead, *The Noble Hustle*

What not to expect when you are expecting.
>   —Katie Roiphe, *The Power Notebooks*

Bab's baby walks at seven months, waywayway!
>   —James Joyce, *Finnegans Wake*

Every man who has changed a diaper has felt impelled . . . to write a book about it.
>   —Barbara Ehrenreich, *The Worst Years of Our Lives*

Diaper backwards spells repaid.
>   —Marshall McLuhan

Having children is *nice*. What a great victory to be *not-nice*.
>   —Sheila Heti, *Motherhood*

Goat curry and a female librarian—that's what I'm in the mood for.
>   —Ben Katchor, *Julius Knipl, Real Estate Photographer*

I've always fantasized about library congress. Let's do it in the HQ 70s.
>   —Alison Bechdel, *Dykes to Watch Out For*

The pleasures of open stacks—with their erotically charged corridors.

—Edmund White, *The Unpunished Vice*

InterLibrary Loan is my sexual preference.

—Wayne Koestenbaum

I was the town librarian, less a woman than a piece of civic furniture.

—Elizabeth McCracken, *The Giant's House*

People can lose their lives in libraries. They ought to be warned.

—Saul Bellow

She had that gaunt full-hipped Appalachian stance.

—Jayne Anne Phillips, *Black Tickets*

Outside every thin woman is a fat man trying to get in.

—Katharine Whitehorn

That dark day when a man decides he must wear his belt under instead of over his cascading paunch.

—Peter De Vries

Fuck love and just get fat.

—Andrew Sean Greer, *Less*

She's fat, but she's *hard*, like a table!

—James Dickey, about his wife, Maxine

If you're not at the table, you're on the menu.

> —Origin unknown

To write a short story you have to be able to stay up all night.

> —Lorrie Moore, *Paris Review* interview

Just start at page one and write like a son of a bitch.

> —Jim Harrison, *Paris Review* interview

No one asked you to be happy. Get to work!

> —Colette

If you want what the syllables want, just do your job.

> —Charles Wright, "A Bad Memory Makes You a Metaphysician,
> a Good One Makes You a Saint"

I'm sure the neighbors think I'm potty but after all—they can hardly haul me off to the bin for scribble scribble scribble.

> —Jean Rhys, letter

Woik! Woik! Woik!

> —Donald Hall, quoting his grandfather, *A Carnival of Losses*

A small daily task, if it be really daily, will beat the labours of a spasmodic Hercules.

> —Anthony Trollope, *An Autobiography*

The art of writing is the art of applying the seat of the pants to the seat of the chair.

> —Mary Heaton Vorse

First forget *inspiration*. Habit is more dependable.

> —Octavia E. Butler, "Furor Scribendi"

The work is finished when you fall over.

> —David Hockney, in *The New York Times*

To be stupid, and selfish, and to have good health are the three requirements for happiness—though if stupidity is lacking, the others are useless.

> —Julian Barnes, *Flaubert's Parrot*

I am not in favor of imposing happiness on people. Everyone has a right to his bad wine, to his stupidity, and to his dirty fingernails.

> —Milan Kundera, *The Farewell Party*

Fleeting, dependent on circumstances, and a bit bovine.

> —Jeanette Winterson, on happiness, *Why Be Happy When You Could Be Normal?*

"Happy" was a word for sorority girls and clowns, and those were two distinctly fucked-up groups of people.

> —Emma Straub, *Modern Lovers*

Hell, I've been teeing off on clowns my whole life.

> —Ralph Ellison, *Trading Twelves: The Selected Letters of Ralph Ellison and Albert Murray*

I'm Ai'ight. You're Ai'ight.

> —Paul Beatty, *The Sellout*

I laced the cocktails with Benzedrine, which I find always makes
a party go.

—Henry Chapman, *Chips: The Diaries of Sir Henry Channon*

I don't think heterosexual parties are workable.

—Christopher Isherwood, *The Sixties: Diaries 1960–1969*

A literary party—over-furnished minds in an under-furnished room.

—Kenneth Tynan, "A Memoir of Manhattan"

An alcoholic is someone you don't like who drinks as much as you
do.

—Dylan Thomas

A narcissist is someone better-looking than you are.

—Gore Vidal

Egotist: A person of low taste, more interested in himself than me.

—Ambrose Bierce

Hubris? him? what did he have to be hubrid about?

—Stanley Elkin, *The MacGuffin*

If you ask where is the Picasso of England or the Ezra Pound of
France, there is only one probable answer: still in the trenches.

—Robert Hughes, *The Spectacle of Skill*

We can forgive you for killing our children. But we will never
forgive you for making us kill yours.

—Golda Meir, to Anwar Sadat

Let me say before I go any further that I forgive nobody.

    —Samuel Beckett, *Malone Dies*

I never forgive but I often forget.

    —Hugh Trevor-Roper

She smelled like I would imagine a mermaid would smell.

    —Gregg Allman, on Cher, *My Cross to Bear*

I have heard the mermaids singing, each to each.
I do not think that they will sing for me.

    —T. S. Eliot, *The Love Song of J. Alfred Prufrock*

Given a fair field in early youth I suspect I might have become
a pretty serious homosexual.

    —Iris Murdoch, *Living on Paper*

In homosexual sex you know exactly what the other person
is feeling.

    —William S. Burroughs

Jesus was a single gentleman.

    —Larry Kramer, *The American People, Volume Two*

Gratitude is my chief erotic emotion.

    —Edmund White, *Inside a Pearl*

I'll be the Lexus lesbian with a flat tire, and you be the surly biker
who stops to help.

    —Alison Bechdel, *Dykes to Watch Out For*

He was the kind of guy I'd rob banks for.

> —David Wojnarowicz, *Close to the Knives*

I'm very fond of my food.

> —W. H. Auden, *Paris Review* interview

Whatever is put in front of me, foodwise, will usually get a
five-star review.

> —Zadie Smith, *Feel Free*

There is only one recipe—to care a great deal for the cookery.

> —Henry James, *Selected Letters*

T. Eliot is toilet spelled backwards.

> —Samuel Beckett, letter

Tea Ass Eliot.

> —Lawrence Ferlinghetti, *Little Boy*

A damned good poet and a fair critic; but he can kiss my ass
as a man.

> —Ernest Hemingway, on T. S. Eliot, letter

My God, ma'am, you're so pretty I'd walk ten miles barefooted on
a freezing morning to stand in your shit.

> —Richard Brautigan, *The Abortion*

Clumps of magic shat out by our errors.

> —Lucia Perillo, "Lubricating the Void"

May cowshit stand up and walk.

—Henry Dumas, "Double Nigger"

Doesn't that liquidate your bowels?

—Ralph Ellison, letter

I could be myself with Miriam, vent my gas, kiss with a bad taste in my mouth, grunt over my bowels on the toilet.

—Stanley Elkin, *The Dick Gibson Show*

I always go for nutters (and they always go for me).

—Angela Carter, letter to Anthony Burgess

You know your trouble, Raven, you don't hold your fork quite right.

—A headmaster to Simon Raven

Vulgar, but not as vulgar as Louis Vuitton, thought Sherman.

—Tom Wolfe, *The Bonfire of the Vanities*

There are people at this table who could vulgarize pure light.

—Robert Stone, *Children of Light*

The kind of people who always go on about whether a thing is in bad taste invariably have very bad taste.

—Joe Orton, in the *Transatlantic Review*

Bad taste is real taste, of course, and good taste is the residue of someone else's privilege.

—Dave Hickey, *Air Guitar*

You're sitting on me style, maybe.

—James Joyce, *Finnegans Wake*

I feel pretty right wing about education.

—Iris Murdoch, *Living on Paper*

I should sooner live in a society governed by the first two thousand names in the Boston telephone directory than in a society governed by the two thousand faculty members of Harvard University.

—William F. Buckley, Jr., *Rumbles Left and Right*

To teach chemistry or psychology or even history or Greek a man must actually know something, but for English nothing seems to be necessary beyond a crude capacity to read and write.

—H. L. Mencken, in *The American Mercury*

Me, fail English? That's unpossible.

—Ralph Wiggum, on *The Simpsons*

However hard you may try, there is never much to say about a henhouse.

—Jose Saramago

The chicken tasted to Flora like distributive injustice personified.

—Nell Zink, *Doxology*

Chubby Checker's chicken-plucker's voice carried distinctly across the crevasse of sub-arctic night.

—John Updike, *Bech: A Book*

And wouldn't you know he'd be a singing man.

  —Toni Morrison, *Beloved*

Oh, you mean the jingle-man!

  —Ralph Waldo Emerson, on Edgar Allan Poe

Tear him for his bad verses, tear him for his bad verses.

  —William Shakespeare, *Julius Caesar*

It is time to strangle several bad poets.

  —Kenneth Koch, "Fresh Air"

Lawn Tennyson, gentleman poet.

  —James Joyce, *Ulysses*

Higher Schlock

  —Greil Marcus, on Leonard Cohen, *Mystery Train*

Looking like I'd spent the last seventy-two hours bobbing for apples
in a vat of Gold Medal flour.

  —Richard Price, on filing a story late

The *things* you can do in that men's room of theirs!

  —Aravind Adiga, on the Union Square Grill bathroom, *Selection Day*

His eyeballs look like he bought them in a joke shop.

  —Denis Johnson, *Jesus' Son*

I generally based appraisals of my affections on the momentary
condition of my genitalia.

  —Nell Zink, *The Wallcreeper*

Whatever chemical change desire is had taken hold.

> —Garth Greenwell, *Cleanness*

It wasn't, in a word, simply that their eyes had met; other conscious organs, faculties, feelers had met as well.

> —Henry James, *The Wings of the Dove*

Henry James was one of the nicest old ladies I ever met.

> —William Faulkner

Like two moist cream cheeses.

> —Edmund Wilson, on feet, *I Thought of Daisy*

A gruyere like a wheel fallen from some barbarian chariot, some Dutch cheeses suggesting decapitated heads smeared in dried blood.

> —Émile Zola, *The Belly of Paris*

Poets have been mysteriously silent on the subject of cheese.

> —G. K. Chesterton

Ah, Wensleydale! The Mozart of cheeses!

> —T. S. Eliot

One of the basic rules of *Esquire* was, if you're going to write about a bear, bring on the bear.

> —Byron Dobell, *Esquire* editor

I enjoyed your article, but I preferred my own.

> —Umberto Eco, to the editor of the *TLS*, after being heavily edited

Death itself is a maw, with, sometimes, a wiggling uvula.

—Charles Foster, *Being a Beast*

The jackal rips out the hare's bowels, but the world rolls on.

—J. M. Coetzee, *Waiting for the Barbarians*

The first thing to know about ground round steak is that it should not be that at all.

—M.F.K. Fisher

A good hamburger should taste like the sound of "Under the Boardwalk."

—Keith Floyd

Eating out a radio.

—Michael Dickman, "Lakes Rivers Streams"

Why was a radio sinful? Lord knows. But it was.
So I had one.

—Reed Whittemore, "The Radio Under the Bed"

In Excelsis Diode.

—Stanley Elkin, *The Dick Gibson Show*

No one of character would make love by it.

—Norman Mailer, on L.A. pop radio, "Superman Comes to the Supermarket"

Nuts to the radio.

—Harold Ross, *Letters from the Editor*

It's funny, isn't it? A shop selling guns, like as if they were carrots and turnips.

—Beryl Bainbridge, *The Girl in the Polka Dot Dress*

The .38 Special which rode under his left armpit like a tumor.

—Robert Penn Warren, *All the King's Men*

Guns make me thirsty.

—Chelsey Minnis, "Showdown"

Like a cherry bomb exploding in me.

—Andy Warhol, on being shot by Valerie Solanas

I'm a real lousy hunter . . . The deer are probably relieved when they smell me and know it's me.

—Larry Brown, *On Fire*

Don't wait to be hunted to hide.

—Samuel Beckett, *Molloy*

If a bullet's going to get you, it's already been fired.

—Ben Fountain, *Billy Lynn's Long Halftime Walk*

I find failure endearing, don't you?

—Max Beerbohm

There's . . . a certain kind of excitement in disgrace.

—Stanley Elkin, *The Dick Gibson Show*

Who wouldn't want to go down in flames?

—John Darnielle, *Wolf in White Van*

There are always a few drops left in the bottle of indignity.

—Andrew Sean Greer, *Less*

There is a kind of snobbery of failure. It's a club, it's the old school, it's Skull and Bones.

—Robert Penn Warren, *All the King's Men*

Nothing amplifies failure like the hug of a stranger.

—Myla Goldberg, *Bee Season*

What demon possessed me that I behaved so well?

—Henry David Thoreau, *Walden*

There's lots of things you never get, Judge, if you wait till you are asked . . . That is why I am not a gentleman, Judge.

—Robert Penn Warren, *All the King's Men*

No nice men are good at getting taxis.

—Katharine Whitehorn

I'm determined to read no more books where the blond-haired women carry away all the happiness.

—George Eliot, *The Mill on the Floss*

I don't want to be a sweetheart. I want to be the fucking love of your life.

—Chimamanda Ngozi Adichie, *Americanah*

Whither thou goest, I will *definitely* go.

> —Fran Ross, *Oreo*

Something fell off the shelf inside her.

> —Zora Neale Hurston, *Their Eyes Were Watching God*

We want you to know that we love you *madly*.

> —Duke Ellington, to a London audience, with bland mockery

—Did you win? he asks.

—It wasn't a match, I say. It was a lesson.

> —Claudia Rankine, *Citizen*

I looked at the phone as if it had been a rattlesnake.

> —Iris Murdoch, *Under the Net*

Men are so wedded to their gadgets . . . It belittles them . . . It takes away all their authority . . . A man ought to give the impression that he's alone.

> —Yasmina Reza, *God of Carnage*

Everybody sounds stoned, because they're e-mailing people the whole time they're talking to you.

> —Jennifer Egan, *A Visit from the Goon Squad*

How can I impress strangers with the gem-like flame of my literary passion if it's a digital slate I'm carrying around, trying not to get it all thumbprinty?

> —James Wolcott, in *Vanity Fair*

She was busted, broke and flat
Had to sell that pussycat.

> —Gillian Welch, "The Way It Goes"

One thing about whoring: It put a chicken on the table.

> —Jeannette Walls, *The Glass Castle*

When the cigarette burns out, time's up.

> —Jodie Foster, in *Taxi Driver*, on sleeping with a john

To all pimps and whores a merry syphilis and a happy gonorrhea.

> —Graham Greene, *The End of the Affair*

Books and harlots have their quarrels in public.

> —Walter Benjamin, *One-Way Street and Other Writings*

What do I know of man's destiny? I could tell you more about radishes.

> —Samuel Beckett, "Enough"

My inner life tends to be measured out in radishes, meat and limes.

> —Jonathan Gold

I beg your parsnips.

> —James Joyce, *Ulysses*

My life like an old turnip: several places at once going bad.

> —Lorrie Moore, *Who Will Run the Frog Hospital?*

A cucumber should be well sliced, and dressed with pepper and vinegar, and then thrown out, as good for nothing.

—Samuel Johnson, in James Boswell's *The Life of Samuel Johnson*

A wise old chef once told me: Wait till peas are in season, then use frozen.

—Fergus Henderson

Is a pea cut in half one wounded thing or two?

—Octavia E. Butler, *Adulthood Rites*

Until they take away my hot dog.

—Seymour Krim, on how long he will keep getting by in literary New York, "For My Brothers and Sisters in the Failure Business"

Only a rank degenerate would drive 1,500 miles across Texas without eating a chicken fried steak.

—Larry McMurtry, *In a Narrow Grave*

Her right hand held a bottle of Pepsi that she'd clogged with salted peanuts and called a late lunch.

—Daniel Woodrell, *Muscle for the Wing*

Like a jar of peanut butter waiting for a thumb.

—Elizabeth Hardwick, on the young women in a Marge Piercy novel

How difficult are our fellow men to digest!

—Frederick Nietzsche, *The Joyous Science*

The sound of Bob Dylan's voice changed more people's ideas about the world than his political message did.

> —Robert Ray, in Greil Marcus's *The History of Rock 'n' Roll in Ten Songs*

The better a singer's voice, the harder it is to believe what they're saying.

> —David Byrne

Whiskey and smoke took all the high notes, now all I can sing is the blues.

> —Jerry Lee Lewis, attributed

I sing in five or six different voices.

> —Axl Rose

The most important of the voices, though, is Devil Woman.

> —John Jeremiah Sullivan, on Axl Rose, *Pulphead*

Those who have a very loud voice are almost incapable of thinking about subtle things.

> —Frederick Nietzsche, *The Joyous Science*

One is prepared for friendship, not for friends.

> —Roberto Bolaño, *Between Parentheses*

Nearly anyone I've found worth knowing was difficult enough, vivid enough, to qualify at some point as my crazy friend.

> —Jonathan Lethem, *The Ecstasy of Influence*

The chances are that if you aren't "difficult" no one will write a book about you.

—Mary-Kay Wilmers, *Human Relations and Other Difficulties*

Friendship is like peeing on yourself: everyone can see it, but only you get the warm feeling that it brings.

—Robert Bloch

New York, killer of poets, do you remember the day you passed me through your lower intestine?

—Karl Shapiro, in *Partisan Review*

Sometimes I feel as if I'm being strangled by the sophisticated scum of New York.

—Charles Wright, *The Messenger*

I'm now making myself as scummy as I can.

—Arthur Rimbaud, letter

At any moment Manhattan could shank you, finish you off.

—Denis Johnson, *The Largesse of the Sea Maiden*

I could stay living in this city if they just installed Blaupunkts in the cabs.

—Bret Easton Ellis, *American Psycho*

Look for rock outcroppings. Manhattan is full of schist.

—Fran Ross, *Oreo*

If there's an intellectual highway, there's also an intellectual subway.
> —Stanley Crouch

When you lead a life of scholarship you can't be bothered with the humorous realities, you know, tits, that kind of thing.
> —Harold Pinter, *Ashes to Ashes*

Genitals are a great distraction to scholarship.
> —Malcolm Bradbury, *Cuts*

He used to put his naked penis on the dinner table, laughing.
> —Maxine Hong Kingston, *Woman Warrior*

I Long to Hold the Poetry Editor's Penis in My Hand
> —Francesca Bell, poem title

What I think about *The New Yorker* can only be expressed like this:
!@!!!@!!!
> —Elizabeth Bishop, letter

Take yir best orgasm, multiply the feeling by twenty, and you're still fuckin miles off the pace.
> —Irvine Welsh, on heroin, *Trainspotting*

Picasso said the smell of opium is the least stupid smell in the world.
> —Jean Cocteau

Two Benadryl were a joke. Like blowing a snot rocket at a forest fire.
> —Ottessa Moshfegh, *My Year of Rest and Relaxation*

I don't take any drugs, I take books.

—Ingeborg Bachmann, *Malina*

Ink, a Drug.

—Vladimir Nabokov, *Bend Sinister*

No pen, no ink, no table, no room, no time, no quiet, no inclination.

—James Joyce, letter to his brother

Get your work done. If that doesn't work, shut up and drink your gin.

—Ray Bradbury, *Paris Review* interview

A deadline is a fine substitute for a genuinely literary urge.

—Anthony Burgess

You lazy cocksucker. I want that Thinkpiece on my desk by Labor Day.

—Hunter S. Thompson, to Anthony Burgess

You're not meant to be doing this. Plenty more where you came from.

—Gore Vidal, on people with writer's block

Now everyone writes just like everyone poops.

—Sigrid Nunez, *The Friend*

If you eat enough books, you start pooping out words.

—Caitlin Moran

At fifty . . . you're as likable as you're going to get.

—Andrew Sean Greer, *Less*

Once you are over fifty they look just over your head as if you were a janitor.

> —Jim Harrison, on women, *The Beast God Forgot to Invent*

It's every woman's tragedy that, after a certain age, she looks like a female impersonator.

> —Angela Carter

And meanwhile time goes about its immemorial work of making everyone look and feel like shit.

> —Martin Amis, *London Fields*

Their dumpling God.

> —Stanley Booth, describing the late Elvis Presley, in *Esquire*

Fat, forty and back.

> —Sex Pistols reunion tour slogan

An invitation is the sincerest form of flattery.

> —Arthur Symons

Two of the saddest words in the English language are "What party?" And L.A. is the "What party" capital of the world.

> —Carrie Fisher

John, I'd love to come to your party, but that would mean I would have to leave my house.

> —Johnny Cash, to John Prine

If you wear a short enough skirt, the party will come to you.

—Dorothy Parker

Milk's a queer arrangement.

—James Joyce, *Finnegans Wake*

You know what milk is? A kind of pus. Think about that, you're guzzling pus.

—Aravind Adiga, *Amnesty*

Damn me, but all things are queer, come to think of 'em.

—Herman Melville, *Moby-Dick*

Queer things always happen in pairs.

—Flann O'Brien, *The Best of Myles*

Sports, politics, and religion are the three passions of the badly educated.

—William H. Gass, *In the Heart of the Heart of the Country*

College football would be much more interesting if the faculty played instead of the students, and even more interesting if the trustees played.

—H. L. Mencken, *Minority Report*

Baseball is a dull game only for those with dull minds.

—Red Smith

Soccer is popular because stupidity is popular.

—Jorge Luis Borges

To the victors belong the spoiled.

—Stanley Elkin, *The Dick Gibson Show*

I don't even know who Mr. Watergate is.

—Vladimir Nabokov, 1974 interview

I'm going to Iowa for an award. Then I'm appearing at Carnegie Hall, it's sold out. Then I'm sailing to France to be honored by the French government—I'd give it all up for one erection.

—Groucho Marx

Take the headache.

—B.B. King, to Buddy Guy, on the side effects of Viagra

This heaven gives me migraine.

—Gang of Four, "Natural's Not in It"

That no one dies of migraine seems, to someone deep into an attack, an ambiguous blessing.

—Joan Didion, "In Bed"

The basic measure of defensive manners is: weed your social garden.

—Quentin Crisp, *Manners from Heaven*

I'll start right now by eliminating you.

—Hattie McDaniel, on being told to eliminate her more "common" acquaintances

If you think squash is a competitive activity try flower arrangement.

—Alan Bennett, *The Complete Talking Heads*

Who described gardening as "the slowest of the performing arts"?

—Frederick Seidel, "To Mac Griswold"

I hate roses. Don't you? It's all right if you can hide them in a cutting garden, but I think a rose garden is the height of ick.

—Cy Twombly, in *Vogue*

The only way I like to see cops given flowers is in a flower pot from a high window.

—Daniel Odier and William S. Burroughs, *The Job*

The best thing to do with a mimeograph is to drop
it from a five story window, on the head of a cop.

—Diane di Prima, "Goodbye Nkrumah"

Their singing is like a train crashing down a high embankment:
a whirlwind of shrieking and banging.

—Anton Chekhov, on the Roma people, *A Life in Letters*

There was Eel Pie Island and a hotel where people had once drunk bottled beer and danced to what Charles Dickens described in *Nicholas Nickleby* as a "locomotive band." Sadly, no recorded evidence of this music survives.

—Elvis Costello, *Unfaithful Music and Disappearing Ink*

If only history were wired for sound.

—Osbert Lancaster, *Afternoons with Baedeker*

Lordy, I hope there are tapes.

—James Comey

Without education, we are in a horrible and deadly danger of taking educated people seriously.

    —G. K. Chesterton

Real education must ultimately be limited to men who insist on knowing. The rest is mere sheep-herding.

    —Ezra Pound

When people don't walk out of my plays I think there is something wrong.

    —John Osborne

Ovations are cheap in America; it's almost as if they stand because they have spent so much money.

    —Patti LuPone

How is it so few can stand a play cold sober?

    —Flann O'Brien, *The Best of Myles*

If you turn that title around you will have an idea of what I thought of that one.

    —Groucho Marx, on Samuel Beckett's *Krapp's Last Tape*

Roget's trollop.

    —What Sylvia Plath called herself when too wordy

A penis with a thesaurus.

    —David Foster Wallace, quoting a friend, on John Updike

I am not a bum or a lecher or a gigolo or some kind of walking penis.

—Philip Roth, *My Life as a Man*

He thought he'd feel like Dustin Hoffman
Driving his penis up to Berkeley.

—Sam Riviere, "Vehicles of Mercy"

The shit they was talking about was too white for me.

—Miles Davis, on dropping out of Juilliard

Does that white skin cover your eyes, too?

—Octavia E. Butler, *Seed to Harvest*

There is no bad luck in the world but whitefolks.

—Toni Morrison, *Beloved*

Sooner or later whitey will take a swing at the left nut of my psyche
and shout "nigger."

—Charles Wright, *Absolutely Nothing to Get Alarmed About*

When you grab me again, whitey, you are going to have two
handfuls of 168 pounds of pure black hell.

—Sam Greenlee, *The Spook Who Sat by the Door*

The Negro has been fucked through the years and in many different
positions in this country.

—Charles Wright, *The Messenger*

Any way they could deprive a Negro was a celebration to 'em.

—Nate Shaw, in *All God's Dangers*

Even black *will* crack if you beat it enough.
  —Roya Marsh, *dayliGht*

I have no gun, but I can spit.
  —W. H. Auden

A lady spat backward upon me by a mistake, not seeing me. But after seeing her to be a very pretty lady, I was not troubled at it at all.
  —Samuel Pepys, diary

Save the rest to grease your cock in case a skunk comes by you want to screw.
  —Ann Beattie, on spit, *Falling in Place*

There were four ice cubes left. I brought up phlegm from my throat and spat on each of the cubes separately. Then I slid the tray back into the freezer.
  —Don DeLillo, *Americana*

I'm not a good person . . . Sorry, that's the way it is.
  —Susan Sontag, *Reborn: Early Diaries, 1947–1963*

When the shooting starts would you rather be armed or legal?
  —Cormac McCarthy, *The Road*

Would Goldilocks have broken into the bears' cottage if she'd seen a sign on the gate that said ARMED RESPONSE?
  —Deborah Levy, *Things I Don't Want to Know*

I found that walking around with a gun in your pants is very different from walking around without a gun in your pants.

—Peter Orner, *Maggie Brown and Others*

I regret the gun was purchased, as it has been a sad obstacle to reading.

—The Reverend John Skinner, diary

I like engineers. They build things that are useful and sometimes beautiful—a brick sewer, a suspension bridge—and take little credit. They do not wear black and designer glasses like architects. They do not crow.

—Rose George, *The Big Necessity*

Science flies you to the moon. Religion flies you into buildings.

—Victor Stenger

Our goddamn Father, who art in heaven, hallowed be thy fucking name.

—Téa Obreht, *Inland*

Martha Stewart contributes more to our civility than the Baptist Church.

—Dave Hickey

Do it in your *own time*, in private, like masturbation.

—Kingsley Amis, on religion

I'll try a pagan friend, thought I, since Christian kindness has proved but hollow courtesy.

—Herman Melville, *Moby-Dick*

There is no God and we are his prophets.

—Cormac McCarthy, *The Road*

Although I reject their proposals, I welcome their advances.

—Edna St. Vincent Millay, on publishers

The two most beautiful words in the English language are "check enclosed."

—Dorothy Parker

Would rather change publisher than title.

—Graham Greene, in a cable to Viking Press, about *Travels with My Aunt*

Fucked and Humiliated would have been a good title, a bit of trash Dostoyevsky.

—Michel Houellebecq, *Serotonin*

She would like her superior intellect to be affirmed in public by the transfer of large amounts of money.

—Sally Rooney, *Normal People*

I had to offer my publisher a bottle that was far too good for him, simply because there was nothing between the insulting and the superlative.

—Yves Mirande, quoted by A. J. Liebling

He stands too near his printer; he corrects the proofs.

—Henry David Thoreau, *The Journals of Henry David Thoreau, 1837–1861*

A forty-fifth reunion is not the best place to come looking for ass.

—Philip Roth, *American Pastoral*

Welcoming a penis just seems more womanly to me than baking chocolate chip cookies or doling out money for a grandchild's college tuition.

—Helen Gurley Brown, *The Late Show*

On some level, I'm always full of Girl Scout cookies.

—Terrance Hayes, "American Sonnet for My Past and Future Assassin"

I remain awkward and uncertain while staying in other people's houses.

—Jenny Diski, *In Gratitude*

If there was one thing I didn't like, it was seeing other people's bedrooms.

—Karl Ove Knausgaard, *My Struggle: Book Four*

Don't talk so much with your mouth.

—Fran Ross, *Oreo*

Does every conversation with you have to be the director's cut?

—Jonathan Lethem, *Motherless Brooklyn*

Try not to talk when you're sober, darling.

—Chelsey Minnis, "Boredom"

Every conversation is a podcast if you close your eyes.

—Karen Chee, on Twitter

And their talk was a refuge.

—Paule Marshall

If this sofa could talk, we'd have to burn it.

—Eudora Welty, in a hotel with Reynolds Price

I had seen Miss Welty buying a frozen pizza at the Jitney Jungle one time.

—Rick Bass, *The Traveling Feast*

Fuck you, fuck pizza, and fuck Frank Sinatra, too.

—Spike Lee, in *Do the Right Thing*

The director recommends that, when the film is shown, a toaster oven containing several heads of garlic be turned on in the rear of the theater, unbeknownst to the audience.

—Les Blank, on how to screen his documentary *Garlic Is as Good as Ten Mothers*

Just for the fun of it, run into a delicatessen and holler out the French name for garlic: *Aiieee.*

—Bruce Jay Friedman, *The Lonely Guy's Book of Life*

No! you won't 'eed nothin' else
But them spicy garlic smells.

—Rudyard Kipling, "Mandalay"

Hell is other people fucking.

—David Gilbert, *And Sons*

I could not take lightly the idea that people made love without me.

—Jean Genet, *The Thief's Journal*

The neighbors in the adjoining room make love . . . every day with a frenzy which makes me jealous . . . I envy people who can scream.

—Marcel Proust

If we keep on fucking, I'm not gonna die.

—Kathy Acker, *Eurydice in the Underworld*

You don't even really give a fuck when we're fucking any more.

—Ali Smith, *Spring*

This isn't going to un-fuck itself.

—Colson Whitehead, *Zone One*

O Florida. O, cold Florida. Could any state be horrida?

—Edna St. Vincent Millay

The whole peninsula of Florida was weighted down with regret. Everyone had left behind a real life.

—Cynthia Ozick, "Rosa"

Nothing down here but scorpions, lizards, vast spiders, mosquitos, vast cockroaches & thorns in the grass.

—Jack Kerouac, letter to Joyce Johnson, in her memoir, *Minor Characters*

A very deep tan is a tricky thing.

—John D. MacDonald, *The Deep Blue Good-By*

Tans are an enemy of sex.

—John Updike, "In Memoriam Felis Felis"

Roll me over on the grill I'm done on this side.

—Lawrence Ferlinghetti, *Little Boy*

When a man gets trouble in his mind
He wanna sleep all the time.

—Bukka White, "Sleepy Man Blues"

I only sleep with people I love, which is why I have insomnia.

—Emilie Autumn

The ideal reader cannot sleep when holding the writer he was
meant to be with.

—Zadie Smith

He awoke at six, as usual. He needed no alarm clock. He was already
comprehensively alarmed.

—Martin Amis, *The Information*

To play against him is like playing against an inebriated kangaroo.

—Ford Madox Ford, on Ezra Pound's tennis game

With a great splashing like a dog retrieving a ball.

—Antonia Fraser, on Harold Pinter's swimming, *Must You Go?*

You can't be deep without a surface.
> —Jonathan Lethem, *You Don't Love Me Yet*

The surface is all you've got. You can only get beyond the surface by working with the surface.
> —Richard Avedon

The body's surface . . . about as serious a thing as there is in life.
> —Philip Roth, *American Pastoral*

It seemed that the face *does* matter, because it affects the man behind it.
> —Garry Wills, *Nixon Agonistes*

Oh God, let me be pretty when I grow up.
> —Jean Rhys, age twelve

The most beautiful faces have some ugly in them.
> —Walter Kirn, *Mission to America*

It's really quite remarkable how complete the illusion is that beauty is the same as goodness.
> —Leo Tolstoy, *The Kreutzer Sonata*

The closest most people get to photographing a friend's central nervous system.
> —James Hamblin, on red eye, *If Our Bodies Could Talk*

Bad news is always true.
> —John Giorno, "Thanx 4 Nothing"

Anything that consoles is fake.

—Iris Murdoch

Prayer's a joke, love a secretion,
the tortured torture, and worse gets worse.

—John Updike, "Spanish Sonnets"

The worst thing you can imagine has already
Zipped up its coat and is heading back
Up the road to wherever it came from.

—Tracy K. Smith, "No-Fly Zone"

He may be dead; or, he may be teaching English.

—Cormac McCarthy

Studying literature at Harvard is like learning about women at
the Mayo Clinic.

—Roy Blount Jr.

Your opinion doesn't matter; you are only a schoolteacher.

—Robert Penn Warren, to Harold Bloom, over dinner

I've seen academic life destroy the best writers of my generation.

—Susan Sontag, *Paris Review* interview

Where psychology meets education
A terrible bullshit is born.

—Ted Pauker, "A Grouchy Good Night to the Academic Year"

For the stories, man, the stories.

> —Charlie Parker, on why he liked country music

Farm emo.

> —Overheard, on country music

Country music is like good grammar. You know it when you hear it, and you know what it's *not*.

> —Dave Hickey, "Dolly Parton's Songs"

Hillybilly stuff is not just music. It's like the New York Stock Exchange. The minute you see a sharp rise in it, you better watch out.

> —James Alan McPherson, "Why I Like Country Music"

Jingobilly.

> —Martin Amis, on the type of music played at Republican conventions

Come Back to the Raft Ag'in, Huck Honey!

> —Leslie Fiedler, essay title

Blow smoke rings
if you can. Or
blow me.

> —James Schuyler, "A Few Days"

It's true, I haven't had head since Eisenhower.

> —Peter Orner, *Maggie Brown and Others*

Speaking in the literature sense, the cop said, grinning, this particular blowjob is going to be a little more Ann Rice than Armistead Maupin.

—Stephen King, *Desperation*

It is little known that I am the only human being in the world who has changed sex and then changed back again.

—Auberon Waugh, *The Diaries of Auberon Waugh*

This is one of the worst things I've ever read—*and I'm crying.*

—Joseph Papp, on Larry Kramer's play *The Normal Heart*

There's the man who murdered all of daddy's friends.

—Larry Kramer, to his dog, every time he passed Ed Koch

I write because I hate. A lot. Hard.

—William Gass, *Paris Review* interview

I tell you, there is such a thing as creative hate!

—Willa Cather, *The Song of the Lark*

Unless I tell you otherwise I am always flipping somebody off.

—Lee Durkee, *The Last Taxi Driver*

Your mania for sentences, my mother said, has dried up your heart.

—Gustave Flaubert, *The Letters of Gustave Flaubert: 1830–1857*

When you write about the people you hate the most, do it with love.

—Hubert Selby, Jr., attributed

Under every friendship there is a difficult sentence that must be said, in order that the friendship can be survived.
    —Zadie Smith, *The Autograph Man*

If one is not to get into a rage sometimes, what is the good of being friends?
    —George Eliot, *Middlemarch*

They had drifted apart, as people do when they promise to stay in touch; the ones who are going to stay in touch don't need to promise.
    —Edward St. Aubyn, *Lost for Words*

It's like seeing Kate Moss take a shit.
    —Ottessa Moshfegh, on her fiction, in *Vice*

Sometimes I'm at stool all night.
    —Hilary Mantel, *Wolf Hall*

Virtually every writer I know would rather be a musician.
    —Kurt Vonnegut, Jr.

Writing about rock & roll . . . ! I mean . . . you know, how indecent can you be?
    —Bob Dylan, radio interview

People pay to see others believe in themselves.
    —Kim Gordon

The men who really believe in themselves are all in lunatic asylums.

—G. K. Chesterton

If you're going to be crazy, you have to get paid for it or else you're going to be locked up.

—Hunter S. Thompson

I want to do with you what spring does with the cherry trees.

—Pablo Neruda, "Every Day You Play"

The trees
Laid their dark arms about the field.

—Alfred, Lord Tennyson, "In Memoriam A. H. H. OBIIT MDCCCXXXIII: 95"

Spring is yea and nay.

—Christina Rossetti, "Summer"

Like pressing your face into wet grass.

—Willem de Kooning, on Larry Rivers's painting

There is too much blank sky where a tree once stood.

—Jesmyn Ward, *Sing, Unburied, Sing*

Turn left by the old house that used to be there before it burned down.

—Robert Creeley, *On Earth*

I am writing with my burnt hand about the nature of fire.

—Ingeborg Bachmann

Smart editors let other people snatch their chestnuts out of the fire for them.

—Jim Comstock, in *The West Virginia Hillbilly*

I was at the end of my rope about people. Widespread travel encourages deepest misanthropy.

—Diane Johnson, *Natural Opium*

Staying in town during the summer is a sin worse than pederasty and sheep-buggering.

—Anton Chekhov, *A Life in Letters*

You feel suddenly—oh, well, all right, I can face this place if I must, as long as there's Penguins.

—Christopher Isherwood, on books, *The Sixties: Diaries 1960–1969*

This then is a book! And there are more of them!

—Emily Dickinson, letter

Republicans think that all over the world
darker-skinned people are having more fun
than they are. It's largely true.

—Jim Harrison and Ted Kooser, *Braided Creek: A Conversation in Poetry*

I had been black for a long time. Before black was beautiful.

—Charles Wright, *Absolutely Nothing to Get Alarmed About*

It's no disgrace to be black, but it's often very inconvenient.

—James Weldon Johnson, *The Autobiography of an Ex-Colored Man*

Many a good book has dark covers.

—Agrippa Hull

Playing the blues in the old days was like being black twice.

—Lightnin' Hopkins

The boogie-woogie rumble
Of a dream deferred.

—Langston Hughes, "Dream Boogie"

A humming ship of voices
big with all
the wrongs done
done them.

—Rita Dove, "Gospel"

Never to have to think of yourself as white is a luxury that makes
you deeply stupid.

—Leonard Michaels, *The Collected Stories*

What is a white person who walks into a James Brown or Sam and
Dave song?

—Amiri Baraka, *Black Music*

White reverb.

—Michael Dickman, "Lakes Rivers Streams"

Save me from bigoted old white bitches.

—Wanda Coleman, "April 15th 1985"

You know how stringy white folks necks gits when dey gits ole.

—Zora Neale Hurston, "Squinch Owl Story"

A writer is like a bean plant—he has his little day, and then
gets stringy.

—E. B. White

It's 10 o'clock at night—do you know where your clitoris is?

—Sign at *Ms.* magazine under Gloria Steinem

I'm going to keep a little clothespin on my clit and then I can pinch
it if I want!

—Terry Southern and Mason Hoffenberg, *Candy*

A clitoral appendage at the mouth of New York's natural harbor.

—Rem Koolhaas, on Coney Island, *Delirious New York*

I don't think he would ever sign a contract with someone fat.
He assigns moral values to fatness.

—Paul Theroux, on V. S. Naipaul

I'm tall and thin . . . but my life is square and small.

—Anne Sexton, *A Self-Portrait in Letters*

No man has ever made a more dramatic demonstration of the aesthetic reasons that people shouldn't get bloated.

> —Pauline Kael, on Robert De Niro's weight gain in *Raging Bull*, *Taking It All In*

Don't be a fathead.

> —Anton Chekhov, *A Life in Letters*

If you won't talk to me I'll write about your face. If you won't look at me I'll write about the back of your head.

> —Roy Blount Jr., *About Three Bricks Shy: And the Load Filled Up*

Research is formalized curiosity.

> —Zora Neale Hurston, "Sweat"

The media. It sounds like a convention of spiritualists.

> —Tom Stoppard, *Night and Day*

A good pun may be admitted among the smaller excellencies of lively conversation.

> —James Boswell, *The Life of Samuel Johnson*

Any man who will not resist a pun will never lie up-pun me.

> —Eve Babitz, *Slow Days, Fast Company*

Coincidences are spiritual puns.

> —G. K. Chesterton

A shrewd person would one day start a religion based on coincidence, if he hasn't already, and make a million.

—Don DeLillo, *Libra*

When I have tense relations with my wife, we speak in Arabic. When we talk business, then we speak English. When our relationship is better, then we talk French.

—Boutros Boutros-Ghali

A black, E white, I red, U green, O blue.

—Arthur Rimbaud, "Vowels"

U R 2 good 2 B 4 got 10.

—Robert Lowell, letter to Elizabeth Bishop

M takes mustard, N drives into town,
O goes to bed with P, and Q drops dead.

—Howard Nemerov, "A Primer of the Daily Round"

Accusing novelists of egotism is like deploring the tendency of champion boxers to turn violent.

—Martin Amis, *The Rub of Time*

Other people. Someone should have told me about them a long time ago.

—Philip Roth, *The Anatomy Lesson*

Nobody, nobody is good enough.

—Joseph Conrad, *Lord Jim*

How fantastically far one is from being humble . . . I want to
be admired.

    —Iris Murdoch, *Living on Paper*

I don't want anything to change, except to be as famous as one can
be, but without that changing anything. Everyone would know in
their hearts that *I* am the most famous person alive—but not talk
about it too much.

    —Sheila Heti, *How Should a Person Be?*

Writerly anti-nonfamous.

    —Joshua Cohen, *Book of Numbers*

I am your number one fan.

    —Kathy Bates, in *Misery*

Mrs. Penniman always, even in conversation, italicized her
personal pronouns.

    —Henry James, *Washington Square*

Everybody has to feel superior to somebody, she said. But it's
customary to present a little proof before you take the privilege.

    —Truman Capote, *Breakfast at Tiffany's*

—May I kiss the hand that wrote *Ulysses*?
—No, it did lots of other things, too.

    —James Joyce's reply

My wang was all I really had that I could call my own.

—Philip Roth, *Portnoy's Complaint*

It was big but it was cuter'n a speckled pup under a red wagon.

—Stanley Elkin, *The Dick Gibson Show*

The tripod.

—Nickname of Henri de Toulouse-Lautrec

The fact is a wire through which one sends a current.

—Saul Bellow

Facts are subversive.

—I. F. Stone

Mimesis—you can't beat it.

—John Updike, *Bech: A Book*

No fact ever contradicted a tree.

—Joshua Cohen, *Book of Numbers*

Who can refute a sneer?

—William Paley

He checks his facts until they weep with boredom.

—Clive James, on Bob Woodward, *Latest Readings*

Some exemplary unpleasant facts are these: that life is short and almost always ends messily; that if you live in the actual world you can't have your own way; that if you do get what you want, it turns out to be not the thing you wanted; that no one thinks as well of you as you do yourself; and that one or two generations from now you will be forgotten entirely and that the world will go on as if you had never existed. Another is that to survive and prosper in this world you have to do so at someone else's expense or do and undergo things it's not pleasant to face: like, for example, purchasing your life at the cost of innocents murdered in the aerial bombing of Europe and the final bombings of Hiroshima and Nagasaki. And not just the bombings. It's also an unpleasant fact that you are alive and well because you or your representatives killed someone with bullets, shells, bayonets, or knives, if not in Germany, Italy, or Japan, then Korea or Vietnam. You have connived at murder, and you thrive on it, and that fact is too unpleasant to face except rarely.

—Paul Fussell, *Thank God for the Atom Bomb*

Gracious Lord, oh bomb the Germans,
Spare their women for Thy Sake,
And if that is not too easy,
We will pardon Thy Mistake.

—John Betjeman, "In Westminster Abbey"

How could the notion that we were modern even arise when people were dropping all around us?

—Karl Ove Knausgaard, *My Struggle: Book Two*

Artists are unreliable; whereas death never lets you down . . . You would buy shares in death, if they were available.

—Julian Barnes, *Nothing to Be Frightened Of*

When I die I want to decompose in a barrel of porter and have it served in all the pubs in Dublin.

—J. P. Donleavy, *The Ginger Man*

How many times do two people have to fuck before one of them deserves to die?

—Don DeLillo, *Cosmopolis*

—How often do you have sex?
—Twice as often as everyone else.

—Ian McEwan, *Guardian* interview

I'm always hawny in the mawnin'.

—Andre Dubus III, *Townie*

We always exuded better sex than we had.

—John Updike, "Midpoint"

That's like foreplay for us. You say cryptic things I don't understand, I give inadequate responses, you laugh at me, and then we have sex.

—Sally Rooney, *Conversations with Friends*

Intercourse is better than no course at all.

—A. R. Ammons, "Analysis Mines and Leaves to Heal"

Better to grasp at straws than not to grasp at all.

—Gish Jen, *The Resisters*

There's a hole in daddy's arm where all the money goes.

—John Prine, "Sam Stone"

I am running out of everything now. Out of veins. Out of money.

—William S. Burroughs

All this work, I complained, is fucking with my high.

—Denis Johnson, *Jesus' Son*

If I could have purchased my medications from a vending machine, I would have paid double for them.

—Ottessa Moshfegh, *My Year of Rest and Relaxation*

What lies will we lie down with tonight?

—Rita Dove, "Beauty and the Beast"

We lie everywhere but on top of each other.

—Rebecca Schiff, *The Bed Moved*

Never to lie is to have no lock to your door.

—Elizabeth Bowen, *The House in Paris*

A little inaccuracy sometimes saves tons of explanation.

—Saki, *The Complete Saki*

Query: Is it possible to cultivate the art of conversation when living in the country all the year round?

—E. M. Delafield, *Diary of a Provincial Lady*

I miss brains, hate this cow life.

—Sylvia Plath, letter

The thing about cows is they're dressed *all in leather*, he said. Head to toe, nothing but leather. It's badass. I mean when you really think about it.

—Rachel Kushner, *The Mars Room*

I want words meat-hooked from the living steer.

—Robert Lowell, "The Nihilist as Hero"

There's a part of me that has never heard of a telephone.

—James Dickey, *Self-Interviews*

A good ole boy can become an intellectual, but an intellectual cannot become a good ole boy.

—James McMurtry, quoting a friend, *Live in Aught-Three*

Shakespeare, the brilliant country boy.

—Delmore Schwartz, "Iago, or the Lowdown on Life"

What someone doesn't want you to publish is journalism; all else is publicity.

—Paul Fussell, *Thank God for the Atom Bomb*

Gall is a basic tool of journalism.

—Hunter S. Thompson, in Juan Thompson's *Stories I Tell Myself*

"I'm on deadline" can get you out of things . . . Whatever kind of work you do, it's always cooler to be on deadline.

—Terry McDonell, *The Accidental Life*

Any man has to, needs to, wants to
Once in a lifetime, do a girl in.

—T. S. Eliot, *Sweeney Agonistes*

I think that if most guys in America could somehow get their fave-rave poster girl in bed and have total license to do whatever they wanted with this legendary body for one afternoon, at least seventy-five percent of the guys in the country would elect to beat her up.

—Lester Bangs

Men often ask me, Why are your female characters so paranoid? It's not paranoia. It's recognition of their situation.

—Margaret Atwood, *Paris Review* interview

If any two people could ever really get inside each other's head, it would scare the pee out of both of them.

—John D. MacDonald, *Dress Her in Indigo*

What one can hide inside one's head and smile.

—Iris Murdoch, *Nuns and Soldiers*

Bad art smells human in all the wrong ways.

—Gertrude Stein, attributed

Enjoying someone else's smell—the most modest form of guilt
there is.

—Francesco Pacifico, *Class*

I know every book of mine by its smell, and I have but to put my nose
between the pages to be reminded of all sorts of things.

—George Gissing

I counted two and seventy stenches,
All well-defined, and several stinks!

—Samuel Coleridge, "Cologne"

The marigold smell of multiple occupancy.

—Elizabeth Hardwick, *The Collected Essays of Elizabeth Hardwick*

All I need to make a comedy is a park, a policeman and a pretty girl.

—Charlie Chaplin

The laughter of unrespectable people having a hell of a fine time.

—James Agee, on silent movie houses, *Agee on Film*

If you can make a reader laugh, he is apt to get careless and go
on reading.

—Henry Green

You have to laugh trouble down to a size where you can talk
about it.

—Dan Jenkins

A sense of humor is just common sense, dancing. Those who lack humor are without judgment and should be trusted with nothing.

   —Clive James

He married a woman to stop her getting away
Now she's there all day.

   —Philip Larkin, "Self's the Man"

He hates women.

   —Jeanette Winterson, on Vladimir Nabokov, *Why Be Happy When You Could Be Normal?*

The knowledge of cooking does not come pre-installed in a vagina.

   —Chimamanda Ngozi Adichie, *Dear Ijeawele*

Cooking created and perpetuated a novel system of male cultural superiority. It is not a pretty picture.

   —Richard Wrangham, *Catching Fire*

Spare me from cooking three meals a day.

   —Sylvia Plath, diary

You are old when the waiter doesn't mention that you are holding the menu upside down.

   —Donald Hall, *A Carnival of Losses*

"Waiter" is such a funny word. It is we who wait.

   —Muriel Spark, *A Good Comb*

There is something triumphant about a really disgusting meal.

   —Laurie Colwin, *Home Cooking*

Do not imagine that Art is something which is designed to give gentle uplift and self-confidence. Art is not a *brassière*.

—Julian Barnes, *Flaubert's Parrot*

The lengthy and rather hysterical debate about the film *Thelma & Louise* . . . was predicated on the idea that stories are supposed to function as instruction manuals.

—Mary Gaitskill, *Somebody with a Little Hammer*

Once you start illustrating virtue, you had better stop writing fiction.

—Robert Penn Warren, *Paris Review* interview

O, a meaning!

—Archibald MacLeish, "Voyage to the Moon"

Show me a plague and I'll show you the world!

—Larry Kramer, *The American People: Volume One*

The friends of the born nurse
are always getting worse.

—W. H. Auden

You can recognize the people who live for others by the haunted look on the faces of the others.

—Katharine Whitehorn

There it sits, fat and awful.

—Iris Murdoch, on her latest novel, in *Living on Paper*

—What's *Augie March* about?

—It's about 200 pages too long.

    —Saul Bellow

Question: Mr. Stoppard, what is your play about? Answer: It's about to make me rich.

    —Tom Stoppard

A straight nose is a great help if one wishes to look serious.

    —Stella Gibbons, *Cold Comfort Farm*

If that's what his face looks like, imagine his scrotum!

    —David Hockney, attributed, on W. H. Auden

It's the kind of face you'd be wearing if your face read the way you felt about the way things were.

    —Robert Coover, *Noir*

To see her in sunlight was to see Marxism die.

    —Harold Brodkey, "Innocence"

To have her meals, and her daily walk, and her fill of novels, and to be left alone, was all that she asked of the gods.

    —Anthony Trollope, *The Eustace Diamonds*

I had neglected to provide myself with books, and as we crept along at the dull rate of four miles per hour, I soon felt the foul fiend Ennui coming upon me.

    —Nathaniel Hawthorne

Boredom slays more of existence than war.

—Norman Mailer, *Paris Review* interview

So boring, he is like a hearse stood up on end.

—Anton Chekhov, *A Life in Letters*

You meet people in your family you'd never happen to run into otherwise.

—Deborah Eisenberg, *Twilight of the Superheroes*

The family religion was judgement.

—David Hare, *The Blue Touch Paper*

Somewhere back along your pedigree—a bitch got over the wall!

—Robert Bolt, *A Man for all Seasons*

It is no use telling me that there are bad aunts and good aunts. At the core, they are all alike. Sooner or later, out pops the cloven hoof.

—P. G. Wodehouse, *The Code of the Woosters*

I'm from the gutter. And don't you ever forget it because I won't.

—Joe Orton, *The Orton Diaries*

The shabbier the snobbier.

—Elaine Dundy, *The Old Man and Me*

At every interval of eating or drinking he played on the table with a fork and knife, like a drumstick.

—An observer, on George Washington

I don't mind if you don't like my manners. I don't like them myself. They are pretty bad. I grieve over them on long winter evenings.

    —Humphrey Bogart, in *The Big Sleep*

Fuck her. I like eating like this.

    —Aravind Adiga, *Amnesty*

I'd listen to the little slurping noises she made as she sucked the liquid in, and I used to hate her for that as for the most heinous act.

    —Leo Tolstoy, *The Kreutzer Sonata*

Conduct! Is conduct everything? One may conduct oneself excellently, and yet break one's heart.

    —Anthony Trollope, *Doctor Thorne*

—Cy Twombly: You would be happy if I just kept well dressed and [had] good manners.

—His mother: What else is there?

    —Quoted in Sally Mann, *Hold Still*

Everybody does have a book in them, but in most cases that's where it should stay.

    —Christopher Hitchens

Your life story would not make a good book. Don't even try.

    —Fran Lebowitz

Write what you know. That should leave you with a lot of free time.

    —Howard Nemerov, attributed

No interviews. No panels. No speeches. No comments. Stay out of the spotlight. It fades your suit.

 —Lew Wasserman

Remarks are not literature.

 —Gertrude Stein

I would trade half of *Childe Harold* for . . . an interview with Byron and all of *Adam Bede* for the same with George Eliot.

 —Wilfrid Sheed, *The Good Word and Other Words*

Don't treat him like God. It wigs him out. Don't dive into his soul, he finds that insulting.

 —Advice given to interviewers by Bob Dylan's office

It's like going around explaining how you sleep with your wife.

 —Philip Larkin, on talking about his writing

Shoes are the first adult machines we are given to master.

 —Nicholson Baker, *The Mezzanine*

Sloanes can become hard of hearing if you're wearing the wrong shoes. How can one really understand a person wearing the wrong shoes?

 —Ann Barr and Peter York, *The Official Sloane Ranger Handbook*

Those who would reject you because you are wearing the wrong shoes are not worth being accepted by.

 —Salman Rushdie, *Joseph Anton*

What was "Cinderella," if not an allegory for the fundamental unhappiness of shoe shopping?

—Elif Batuman, *The Idiot*

To the disinterested, a foot fetishist is ridiculous; right away you imagine a pathetic cringer who works at Thom McAn.

—Mary Gaitskill, *Somebody with a Little Hammer*

I find it hard to relax around any man who's got the second button on his shirt undone.

—Bill Nighy

Love me, love my dirty shirt.

—James Joyce, *Ulysses*

History's meant to be a bummer, not a stroll down memory lane.

—Simon Schama, on *Downton Abbey*

Understanding the past requires pretending that you don't know the present.

—Paul Fussell, *Thank God for the Atom Bomb*

It is difficult at times to repress the thought that history is about as instructive as an abattoir.

—Seamus Heaney, Nobel Prize lecture

The sex act cruelly mimics history's decline and fall.

—Camille Paglia, *Sexual Personae*

The past is always tense and the future, perfect.
　　—Zadie Smith, *White Teeth*

The great drive-in screen of the future.
　　—Gish Jen, *Who's Irish?*

Have you decided yet what historical moment you would have most like to have witnessed with your own eyes and ears?
　　—Padgett Powell, *The Interrogative Mood*

It's a form of terrorism *not* to bomb this town.
　　—Lorrie Moore, *A Gate at the Stairs*

Are you not the color of this country's current threat Advisory?
　　—Terrance Hayes, *American Sonnets for My Past and Future Assassin*

Do you periodically walk around and check to see that "the area is secure"?
　　—Padgett Powell, *The Interrogative Mood*

Terror, no need to add,
Depends on who's wearing the hood.
　　—Roger Woddis, "Ethics for Everyman"

If Americans experience sublimity
the terrorists have won.
　　—Ben Lerner, "Mad Lib Elegy"

I used to think it was possible for an artist to alter the inner life of the culture. Now bomb-makers and gunmen have taken that territory.

—Don DeLillo, *Mao II*

—Fatwa sex?
—The best sex there is.

—Larry David and Salman Rushdie, *Curb Your Enthusiasm*

Charming friends need not possess minds.

—Muriel Spark, *All the Stories of Muriel Spark*

We cherish our friends not for their ability to amuse us, but for ours to amuse them.

—Evelyn Waugh

We do whatever we can to make the other one feel famous.

—Sheila Heti, *How Should a Person Be?*

If you want your book to get a bad review, have a friend do it.

—Christopher Ricks, *Dylan's Visions of Sin*

I don't read my reviews, I measure them.

—Attributed to Joseph Conrad and Arnold Bennett

Class! Yes, it's still here. Terrific staying power, and against all the historical odds.

—Martin Amis, *London Fields*

Class warfare is one of the few interesting or worthwhile areas of politics, of course, keeping the rich on their toes and giving the poor something to think about.

—Auberon Waugh, *The Diaries of Auberon Waugh*

I'd like to see you move up to the goat-class where I think you belong.

—Philip K. Dick, *Do Androids Dream of Electric Sheep?*

All love is socioeconomic. It's the gradients in status that make arousal possible.

—Gary Shteyngart, *The Russian Debutante's Handbook*

[His public school accent] got on my tits like anything.

—Angela Carter

Her accent alone burned a hole in my lower intestines.

—Peter Orner, *Maggie Brown and Others*

Let's buy a castle and murder King Duncan and settle down.

—John Updike, *Bech Is Back*

If you want a piece of property to go downhill, just leave it in the care of a bunch of word people.

—Madeleine Blais, *To the New Owners*

The simple question "What color do you want to paint that upstairs room?" might, if we follow things to their logical conclusions, be stated: "How do I live, knowing that I will one day die and leave you?"

—Donald Antrim, *The Verificationist*

There's nothing that irritates me so much as paying rent.

    —Iris Murdoch, *Under the Net*

One square foot less and it would be adulterous.

    —Robert Benchley, on an office shared with Dorothy Parker

You've got to lie to stay halfway interested in yourself.

    —Barry Hannah

A lie may fool someone else, but it tells you the truth: you're weak.

    —Tom Wolfe, *The Bonfire of the Vanities*

I expect you've got a lot of those goddam maple trees doing their stuff over there.

    —Iris Murdoch, *Living on Paper*

All the trees had dropped acid.

    —Raymond Mungo, *Total Loss Farm*

Show me a woman who cries when the trees lose their leaves in autumn and I'll show you a real asshole.

    —Nora Ephron, *Heartburn*

I say reject both [poems]. The Poplar one is just another tree one to me and, so help me God, I'm for a moratorium on trees for two or three years.

    —Harold Ross, *Letters from the Editor*

The best things in life are free. The second best are very, very expensive.

—Coco Chanel, attributed

The rule is not to talk about money with people who have much more or much less than you.

—Katharine Whitehorn

It's really hard to be roommates with people if your suitcases are much better than theirs.

—J. D. Salinger, *The Catcher in the Rye*

Thank you for this night like a bag of yellow Doritos.

—Veronica Geng, *Love Trouble Is My Business*

Fritos are so nutritious.

—Marianne Moore, to Donald Hall

The greatest meal of my life involved a Triscuit.

—Jonathan Miles, "A Taste for the Hunt"

Has anybody noticed that we haven't won a game since we ate that chicken á la king?

—Jim Bouton, *Ball Four*

I thank God I am a man of low tastes.

—Oliver Wendell Holmes, Jr.

If you happen to catch . . . me in a low dive my excuse is simple: "I'm writing a book."

—Leonard R. N. Ashley, "The Cockney's Hornbook"

Bring us a basin! We're going to be sick!
— Roald Dahl, *Matilda*

Shelley just barfed on a Dodge Colt with a Wellesley College window decal.
— Susan Orlean, *Saturday Night*

He seems to be vomiting someone's taupe pajamas.
— Don DeLillo, *Underworld*

Puking seems to have perked you up.
— Yasmina Reza, *God of Carnage*

Vomit is passionate.
— Norman Mailer, *Cannibals and Christians*

Cough it up, man. Get it out in bits.
— James Joyce, *Ulysses*

You can't really dust for vomit.
— *This Is Spinal Tap*

Bee vomit, he said once
that's all honey is.
— Rita Dove, "In the Old Neighborhood"

Good greaser vomit! Pablo digs good greaser vomit!
— Terry Southern, *Red-Dirt Marijuana*

I want to rise so high that when I shit I won't miss anybody.
— William H. Gass, *In the Heart of the Heart of the Country*

I became a journalist partly so that I wouldn't ever have to rely on the press for my information.

—Christopher Hitchens, *Hitch-22*

You may not be able to change the world, but at least you can embarrass the guilty.

—Jessica Mitford

We like to appear in the newspapers
So long as we are in the right column.

—T. S. Eliot, *The Family Reunion*

Then shall we be news-crammed.

—William Shakespeare, *As You Like It*

One reason cats are happier than people
is that they have no newspapers.

—Gwendolyn Brooks, *In the Mecca*

You are not a nice boy, David . . . Stick to the wicked.

—Philip Roth, to David Hare, about Hare's work

It's not your fate to be well treated, Ignatius cried. You're an overt masochist. Nice treatment will confuse and destroy you.

—John Kennedy Toole, *A Confederacy of Dunces*

Between two evils, I always pick the one I have never tried before.

—Mae West

Red or white?

> —The three most depressing words in the English language, according
> to Kingsley Amis

My idea of a fine wine was one that merely stained your teeth
without stripping the enamel.

> —Clive James

Black Boy,
beware of wine labels,
for the Republic does not guarantee
what the phrase "Château Bottled" means.

> —Melvin B. Tolson, "PSI"

I don't like my wine in capsules.

> —Gioacchino Rossini, on grapes

I wish we had some more glasses of arbor vitae.

> —James Joyce, *Finnegans Wake*

Half the world is redoing its kitchens, the other half is starving.

> —Don DeLillo, *Zero K*

We weren't poor, we just didn't have any money.

> —Thomas Hart Benton, attributed

A way of keeping yourself feeling rich and civilized even when
you're quite poor.

> —Marie Ponsot, on reading poetry

The rich can afford to be virtuous, the poor must shift as best they can.

    —Angela Carter, *The Sadeian Woman*

That is one of the bitter curses of poverty; it leaves no right to be generous.

    —George Gissing

I make a lunge for the dollar, the eagle flies in the opposite direction.

    —Charles Wright, *The Messenger*

He calls them shithawks.

    —Lucia Perillo, on eagles, quoting a friend, "Serotonin"

When I hear a man talk of Sound Finance, I know him for an enemy of the people.

    —Hyde Park orator, in *Geoffrey Madan's Notebooks*

He did not follow the fat gods.

    —Saul Bellow

Never trust a fart. Never pass up a drink. Never ignore an erection.

    —Walter Cronkite's rules for old men, via Roger Angell

The Queen's fart.

    —Silent method of opening a champagne bottle

An imperfectly suppressed fart.

    —John Barth, on what the word "spoof" sounds like

I remember you, you came in my mouth and it tasted like
strawberries.

 —Jim Carroll, *The Basketball Diaries*

He looked up from his fried chicken and said, I just want to die with
a big dick in my mouth.

 —David Wojnarowicz, *Close to the Knives*

The trouble with this country is that a man can live his entire life
without knowing whether or not he is a coward.

 —John Berryman, to James Dickey

Every man thinks meanly of himself for not having been a soldier,
or not having been at sea.

 —Samuel Johnson

I like a look of Agony,
Because I know it's true.

 —Emily Dickinson

When I died they washed me out of the turret with a hose.

 —Randall Jarrell, "The Death of the Ball Turret Gunner"

This Room and This Gin and These Sandwiches

 —Edmund Wilson, play title

Gin thou wert mine awn thing.

 —John Gay, *The Beggar's Opera*

I'm Saving My Blackheads for You

    —Loudon Wainwright III, song title

My lungs are thick with the smoke
of your absence.

    —Raymond Carver, "A Forge, and a Scythe"

Your body is opium and you are its only true smoker.

    —Brenda Shaughnessy, "Your One Good Dress"

I was the kind of pothead who looked like a small cloud being
propelled by a pair of legs.

    —Clive James, *Latest Readings*

When I was a kid, I inhaled frequently. That was the point.

    —Barack Obama

No smoking in bars. What next, no fucking in bars?

    —Kim Cattrall, in *Sex in the City*

Even the smell of tobacco made a man more rational.

    —Aravind Adiga, *Amnesty*

Then, worst of all, the anxious thought,
Each time my plane begins to sink
And the No Smoking sign comes on:
What will there be to drink?

    —W. H. Auden, "On the Circuit"

Smokeless and breadless, we face a bad weekend.

    —Dylan Thomas, *Selected Letters of Dylan Thomas*

If there is hope, wrote Winston, *it lies in the proles.*

    —George Orwell, *Nineteen Eighty-Four*

Fred Astaire represents the aristocracy when he dances, and I represent the proletariat.

    —Gene Kelly

We can't all be proletarians, you know.

    —Dwight Macdonald, letter

Reverse snobbery, unlike the traditional kind, is a tribute to democracy—it's egalitarianism overshooting the mark.

    —Michael Kinsley, "O'Reilly Among the Snobs"

My place comfortable in the lowerarchy.

    —A. R. Ammons, "Hibernaculum"

Where do people like us live?

    —Bruce Springsteen's parents, to a gas station attendant, upon arriving in California, in his *Born to Run*

But the peasants. How do the peasants die?

    —Leo Tolstoy's last words, attributed

Haven't you noticed that every time the government fucks up McDonald's has a new sandwich?

    —Bill Burr

The last thing I ever wanted was to be alive when the three most powerful men on the whole planet would be named Bush, Dick and Colon.

—Kurt Vonnegut, Jr., *A Man Without a Country*

No baby knows when the nipple is pulled from his mouth for the last time.

—Jonathan Safran Foer, *Here I Am*

My nipples are like the teats of a rain-god.

—Jeanette Winterson, *Frankissstein*

The majesty of a nipple not yet touched.

—A. R. Ammons, "The Gathering"

The Nipple.

—What regulars call the NYPL (New York Public Library)

For manual workers nipples are a trial. One has to sandpaper the hauns before going to bed with one's woman.

—James Kelman, *You Have to Be Careful in the Land of the Free*

I think he's a natural playwright. He writes by sanded fingertips.

—Lillian Hellman, on Tennessee Williams

People who like quotes love meaningless generalizations.

—Graham Greene

Life itself is a quotation.

—Jorge Luis Borges

One has to secrete a jelly in which to slip quotations down people's throats and one always secretes too much jelly.

—Virginia Woolf

They dug each other's references and felt smarter in each other's presence.

—Chris Kraus, *I Love Dick*

What is that unforgettable line?

—Samuel Beckett, *Happy Days*

It is invariably oneself that one collects.

—Jean Baudrillard

The premonition of apocalypse springs eternal in the human breast.

—Irving Kristol, *On the Democratic Idea in America*

Who opens the morning papers without the wild hope of huge headlines announcing another great disaster? Provided of course that it affects other people and not oneself.

—Iris Murdoch, *A Fairly Honourable Defeat*

A sliver off the comet of the American chaos had come loose.

—Philip Roth, *American Pastoral*

I just like people with some Looney Tune in their souls.

—Lester Bangs, *Psychotic Reactions and Carburetor Dung*

They don't have any gizzards. We had gizzards, man.

> —Roy Blount Jr., quoting Dwight White of the Pittsburgh Steelers on the bland teams that followed his, *About Three Bricks Shy: And the Load Filled Up*

Those whom the Gods wish to destroy, they probably begin by calling "charismatic."

> —Christopher Hitchens, *And Yet*

I'm an alcoholic, goddamn it!

> —Dwight Macdonald, when asked why he drank so much, *A Moral Temper: The Letters of Dwight Macdonald*

I hereby charge and assert that the testy but lovable Boswell who annotates by old laundry slips, Dwight Macdonald, drinks tea.

> —Tom Wolfe, letter to the editor, in *The New York Review of Books*

The fact is you're a shocking wreck.

> —Franz Wright, "Alcohol"

Hubcap ripping and parked-car creeping, dime-store clipping and window peeping.

> —Chuck Berry, on petty crime, *The Autobiography*

I love the con, crises are my fuel.

> —Clancy Sigal, *Black Sunset*

Faint heart never fucked a pig.

> —Philip Prowse, attributed

Why not steal a fish from the market to make you bolder?
—Deborah Levy, *Hot Milk*

Don't buy. Steal. If you act like it's yours, no one will ask you to pay for it.
—Jerry Rubin, *Do It*

Nobody steals books but your friends.
—Roger Zelazny, *The Guns of Avalon*

My friends have signed copies of my books that I did not sign.
—Gabriel García Márquez, *The Scandal of the Century*

There are no innocent bystanders. What are they doing there in the first place?
—William S. Burroughs, *My Education*

Somebody always leaves a banana-skin on the scene of a tragedy.
—Graham Greene, *Our Man in Havana*

If you want to know who your friends are, get yourself a jail sentence.
—Charles Bukowski, *Notes of a Dirty Old Man*

My friends don't seem to be friends at all but people whose phone numbers I haven't lost.
—Nick Hornby, *High Fidelity*

How many women can you butt-dial in one evening!
—Frederick Seidel, "Abusers"

Should I have butt implants? Are my tits pointing in the right direction?

> —Rupert Everett, *Red Carpets and Other Banana Skins*

Old friends are almost indistinguishable from enemies.

> —Cyril Connolly, *The Unquiet Grave*

We hate old friends: we hate old books: we hate old opinions; and at last we come to hate ourselves.

> —William Hazlitt

There is a time for loyalty and a time when loyalty comes to an end.

> —Muriel Spark, *A Good Comb*

War is the truest form of divination.

> —Cormac McCarthy, *Blood Meridian*

What's the line? War is God's way of teaching Americans geography.

> —Lisa Halliday, *Asymmetry*

In the end, really, there's nothing much to say about a true war story, except maybe "Oh."

> —Tim O'Brien, *The Things They Carried*

Alienation is when your country is at war, and you want the other side to win.

> —*Ramparts* magazine headline, 1969

As I write, highly civilized human beings are flying overhead, trying to kill me.

    —George Orwell, *The Lion and the Unicorn*

This morning the sky was a ceiling of airplanes.

    —Colette

There's a time for reciting poems, and a time for fists.

    —Roberto Bolaño, *The Savage Detectives*

But, oh Viv, right doesn't make might.

    —Ken Kesey, *Sometimes a Great Notion*

You can't be a **Real Country** unless you have **A BEER** and an **airline**—it helps if you have some kind of a *football team*, or some *nuclear weapons*, but *at the very least* you need **A BEER**.

    —Frank Zappa, *The Real Frank Zappa Book*

He's so dumb he thinks cunnilingus is an Irish airline.

    —Arno Schmidt

Two and a half minutes of squelching.

    —Johnny Rotten's definition of sex

And consummation comes, and jars two hemispheres.

    —Thomas Hardy, "The Convergence of the Twain"

An editor is a man who doesn't know what he wants but recognizes it instantly.

    —William E. Rae, attributed, in Terry McDonell's *The Accidental Life*

If it's the writer's book, it's the editor's magazine.

> —Robert Gottlieb, *Avid Reader*

Writers can handle fast rejection. But they cannot stand the slow no. Whenever I receive copy I feel there's a time bomb in my bag.

> —Tina Brown, *The Vanity Fair Diaries*

One who reads the script overnight.

> —How David Hare judges a great agent or producer, in *The Blue Touch Paper*

When she was not the glacier, she was the narrow Alpine pass.

> —Brendan Gill, on Katherine White's editing, *Here at The New Yorker*

Ah, my friend, I sometimes think that I lead a highly dangerous life, since I'm *one of those machines that can burst apart!*

> —Frederick Nietzsche

You would think by now we could just go poof.

> —Lucia Perillo, "Time Will Clean the Carcass Bones"

The world keeps ending but new people too dumb to know it keep showing up as if the fun's just started.

> —John Updike, *Rabbit Is Rich*

Either forswear fucking others or the affair is over.

> —First sentence of Philip Roth's *Sabbath's Theater*

The plural of spouse is spice.

> —Christopher Morley

If truth were everywhere to be shown, a scarlet letter would blaze forth on many a bosom.

> —Nathaniel Hawthorne, *The Scarlet Letter*

For most people, [affairs] are the *only* creative adventures they'll ever have.

> —Eve Babitz, *Slow Days, Fast Company*

A scandal was after all a sort of service to the community.

> —Saul Bellow, *Herzog*

If it were possible for a book to give a physical stink off its pages, this one would.

> —George Orwell, on Dalí's memoir, in "Benefit of Clergy: Some Notes on Salvador Dalí"

The air smelled like disinfectant and something else that was meant to be killed by disinfectant.

> —Denis Johnson, *The Largesse of the Sea Maiden*

His colon was probably spastic. He was dyspeptic, fitful, an alimentary type. He often reeked of Maalox.

> —Chang-rae Lee, *Native Speaker*

If most of us abhor shit, it is because most of us are a little hideous inside.

> —Norman Mailer, *Cannibals and Christians*

Where there is a stink of shit there is a smell of being.

> —Antonin Artaud

The Pittsburgh Pirates shout because they won
and in a sense we're all winning
we're alive.

—Frank O'Hara, "Steps"

Pirates could happen to anyone.

—Tom Stoppard, *Rosencrantz and Guildenstern Are Dead*

Pandemonium! What a great thing football is, that it allows us at
rare moments to be pandemonious.

—Roy Blount Jr., *About Three Bricks Shy: And the Load Filled Up*

Rooting is in our blood; we take sides as we take breaths.

—Janet Malcolm, *Iphigenia in Forest Hills*

Sports constitute a code, a language of the emotions, and a tourist
who skips the stadiums will not recoup his losses at Lincoln Center
and Grant's Tomb.

—Wilfrid Sheed

Imagine Lou Gehrig with a beard! Jackie Robinson! Babe Ruth!
Ted Williams!

—Donald Hall, *A Carnival of Losses*

Real American crazy shit. America amok! America amuck!

—Philip Roth, *American Pastoral*

Craziness, down through history, has performed impressively.

—John Updike, *Bech Is Back*

Justice?—You get justice in the next world; in this world you have the law.

—William Gaddis, *A Frolic of His Own*

Evidently, to be a good trial lawyer you have to be a good hater. A lawsuit is to ordinary life what war is to peacetime.

—Janet Malcolm, *The Journalist and the Murderer*

I don't want to know what the law is, I want to know who the judge is.

—Roy Cohn

I believe that if ever I had to practice cannibalism, I might manage it if there were enough tarragon around.

—James Beard

For all his tattooings he was on the whole a clean, comely looking cannibal.

—Herman Melville, *Moby-Dick*

—I wish my tattoos were gone, Jessica said . . .
—There is a way, said Lila. But it involves sex.

—Nicholson Baker, *House of Holes*

Fug you. Fug the goddam gun.

—Norman Mailer, *The Naked and the Dead*

So you're the young man who can't spell *fuck*.

—Tallulah Bankhead, to Norman Mailer, attributed

Fik yew!

—James Joyce, *Finnegans Wake*

Has he ever used the search term "teen"?

—Sally Rooney, *Conversations with Friends*

The thousand sordid images
Of which your soul was constituted.

—T. S. Eliot, "Preludes"

I hate you, God, I hate You as though You existed.

—Graham Greene, *The End of the Affair*

He *thought* he was the son of God, he disliked his parents, was a prig [and] where was he, what was he doing, between the ages of twelve and twenty-nine?

—Cyril Connolly, on Jesus, in *The Unquiet Grave*

Sunday is the most segregated day of the week.

—Martin Luther King, Jr.

It should be different from another day. People may walk; but not throw stones at birds.

—Samuel Johnson, on Sundays

For every bird there is a stone thrown at a bird.

—Maggie Smith, "Good Bones"

He was of the faith chiefly in the sense that the church he currently did not attend was Catholic.

—Kingsley Amis, *One Fat Englishman*

Every man with a bellyful of the classics is an enemy of the
human race.
>—Henry Miller, *Tropic of Cancer*

The thing about books is, there are quite a number you don't have
to read.
>—Donald Barthelme

Anyone who's read all of Proust plus *The Man Without Qualities* is bound
to be missing out on a few other titles.
>—Lorrie Moore, *A Gate at the Stairs*

I read assiduously. I kept up with my species.
>—Leonard Michaels, *Sylvia*

The only thing left to people in their despair was reading.
>—Michel Houellebecq, *Submission*

Reading is a majority skill but a minority art.
>—Julian Barnes, *Through the Window*

Nobody knows how to feel and they're checking around for hints.
>—Don DeLillo, *Mao II*

—How do you know all this?
—I'm a fucking librarian.
>—Jenny Offill, *Weather*

I take note of the way people act when they're around mirrors.

—Helen Oyeyemi, *Boy, Snow, Bird*

I haven't enjoyed a mirror since 1994.

—Kevin Barry, *Night Boat to Tangier*

Let us be grateful to the mirror for revealing to us our appearance only.

—Samuel Butler, *Erewhon*

When God gave us mirrors, he had no idea.

—My Morning Jacket, "Librarian"

I don't want to look as if I have been piloting the Concorde without a windshield.

—Christopher Hitchens, on face-lifts, *And Yet*

—How old does she look after her facelift?
—A very old twelve.

—Noël Coward's reply, attributed

The More You Ignore Me, the Closer I Get.

—Morrissey, song title

Blameless people are always the most exasperating.

—George Eliot, *Middlemarch*

Twitter is a simple service for smart people, Facebook is a smart service for simple people.

—Jonah Peretti

Oh, how I hated all of them. Through gritted teeth I pressed "like" on all their posts, pretty much without exception.

—Keith Gessen, *A Terrible Country*

Pellet of affection! Pellet of rage!

—Jenny Offill, *Weather*

Like. Like. Like! The babble of this subculture is drowning me!

—Gore Vidal, *Myra Breckinridge*

Intent of her phone, reading, tapping, frowning in the contemporary manner.

—Ian McEwan, *The Children Act*

YouTube, my shame kiln.

—Wayne Koestenbaum, *Humiliation*

Five hundred million sentient people entrapped in the recent careless thoughts of a Harvard sophomore.

—Zadie Smith, on Facebook, "Generation Why?"

Just me and my id, hanging out, clicking.

—Anna Wiener, *Uncanny Valley*

A dozen to begin with. After that, we'll see.

—Colette, on being overcome by the scent of a passing plate of shrimp, *Claudine in Paris*

I shall be but a shrimp of an author.

—Thomas Gray

One of the best ways of annoying a prawn is simply to put it in the middle of a room and laugh at it.

—Auberon Waugh, *The Diaries of Auberon Waugh*

When a writer is born into a family, the family is finished.

—Czesław Miłosz

He was one of those people who can chew their grievances like a cud.

—George Orwell, *The Road to Wigan Pier*

I must express some relief that her memoirs did not proceed to me.

—Elizabeth Hardwick, on Mary McCarthy, *The Collected Essays of Elizabeth Hardwick*

Telling funny stories about your friends is a tricky business if you intend to go on having friends.

—Mary-Kay Wilmers, *Human Relations and Other Difficulties*

I am the nemesis of the would-be forgotten.

—Saul Bellow, *Herzog*

I like a view but I like to sit with my back turned to it.

—Gertrude Stein, *The Autobiography of Alice B. Toklas*

He liked subtle scenery, not the brass bands of it.

—Kenneth Clark

Just as a bank won't lend you money unless you are too rich to need it, exercise is a pastime only for those who are already slender and physically fit.

    —Christopher Hitchens, *And Yet*

People looked after their cars better than they looked after their bodies.

    —Rachel Cusk, *Kudos*

Improves one's posture but not one's tranquillity.

    —Angela Carter, on yoga

A few weeks without my trainer dragging me out of bed at six, a few forgotten visits to Louis Licari, in two months I would be a big girl in thick glasses with a bushy ponytail. How lovely that sounds.

    —Tina Brown, *The Vanity Fair Diaries*

Doc, all my life people say I was ugly. Makes me feel mean.

    —Boris Karloff, in *The Raven*

Her face was as useless to her as hot stew.

    —Diane Williams, *The Collected Stories of Diane Williams*

Why does your face resemble the underside of a colander in which wet lettuce is heaped?

    —John Updike, *Bech: A Book*

Desire makes us ugly unless the other person is lost to it too.

    —Dana Spiotta, *Innocents and Others*

As ugly as you is, the trees leanin over away from you.

—Henry Dumas, "Double Nigger"

I'm the fortieth-ugliest man in this bar.

—Gary Shteyngart, *Super Sad True Love Story*

Sugar, I know I'm a funny lookin' fella. Wooo, but if I clean up won't you have a little pity on me?

—Lightnin' Hopkins, "Big Black Cadillac Blues"

They eat green salad and drink human blood.

—Saul Bellow, on women, *Herzog*

I don't like the way he writes about women, and I don't like the way I sound complaining about it.

—Nell Freudenberger, on Philip Roth

—Kate, you've never read my books. They're *all* about women.
—Yes, she said, but coldly observed. As if extraterrestrial life.

—John Updike, *Bech: A Book*

The dawn of space travel is the dawn of woman.

—Samuel R. Delany, *Stars in My Pockets Like Grains of Sand*

Even in space there's a double standard for women.

—Carrie Fisher

I'm sorry that astronaut will be brought back from her own chosen heaven.

—Octavia E. Butler, *Parable of the Sower*

Nothing ill come near thee!
>—William Shakespeare, *Cymbeline*

The ideal way to get rid of any infectious disease would be to shoot instantly every person who comes down with it.
>—H. L. Mencken

Meanwhile a deer tick slides into the very last reserved parking spot.
>—Michael Dickman, "Lakes Rivers Streams"

How many ticks are *on* this wood?
>—Frederick Nietszche, *The Joyous Science*

Before Instagram it was so much harder to figure out exactly how much money people have.
>—Emily Gould, on Twitter

My hair almost stands on end when I remember the debts I have gotten into.
>—Anton Chekhov, *A Life in Letters*

I don't know what happened about the money but I'm most awfully sorry.
>—Jean Rhys, *The Letters of Jean Rhys*

People were paying with bills they'd made by tearing a corner off a twenty and pasting it onto a one.
>—Denis Johnson, *Jesus' Son*

Algebra and money are essentially levelers, the first intellectually, the second effectively.

—Simone Weil, *Gravity and Grace*

Money is sad shit.

—Richard Brautigan, *The Edna Webster Collection of Undiscovered Writing*

I like the social tradition that we must not poke a fire in a friend's drawing-room unless our friendship dates back full seven years.

—Max Beerbohm, *The Prince of Minor Writers*

When he planned to visit a friend in an apartment building new to him, he went so far as to secure blueprints of the building and ascertain the position of its fire escapes.

—Brendan Gill, on the cartoonist Alan Dunn, who feared fire,
   Here at The New Yorker

Each one of us will trail a sinuous hose. It will not be filled with water. It will be filled with oil.

—Max Beerbohm, on his dream fire department, *The Prince of Minor Writers*

When he bought a cornet he'd shine it up and make it glisten like a woman's leg.

—Michael Ondaatje, *Coming Through Slaughter*

Yes, that "unmistakable" Laurel Canyon sound. The sound of Laurel Canyon is entertainment lawyers screaming at their dogs.

—Father John Misty

Even the best of us are at least part-time bastards.
—Mary Karr

I don't want every one to like me; I should think less of myself if some people did.
—Henry James, *The Portrait of a Lady*

Time misspent in youth is sometimes all the freedom one ever has.
—Anita Brookner, *A Misalliance*

Freedom isn't speaking your mind freely. Freedom is having the money to go to Mexico.
—Nell Zink, *Mislaid*

Rock and roll means well, but it can't help telling young boys lies.
—The Drive-By Truckers, "Marry Me"

Don't you think women would be happier if "Layla" had a whole chorus about Eric Clapton watching Patti Boyd trying to climb over a park fence, pissed, in order to retrieve a shoe she threw in there for a bet?
—Caitlin Moran, *How to Be a Woman*

Normally in the presence of lack of greatness, I would focus on the bassist's arms.
—Rebecca Schiff, *The Bed Moved*

The word "semiotics" was always a tip-off: head for the hills!
—Clive James, *Latest Readings*

If he's so clever, why doesn't he write a novel of his own?

    —Angela Carter, on Jacques Derrida

The plywood of Academe.

    —Gore Vidal, "Ford's Way"

He has a certain syrup but it does not pour.

    —Gertrude Stein, on Glenway Wescott

I wanted to take that cat to a hot pan and sear its foul backside in an explosion of oil.

    —Claire-Louise Bennett, *Pond*

I know about dogs; but how, pray, does one kick a cat's ass?

    —Ralph Ellison, to Saul Bellow, *The Selected Letters of Ralph Ellison*

Zigzagging after cats and that.

    —Anthony Burgess, *A Clockwork Orange*

Interior desecrators and natural downholsterers.

    —Patrick Leigh Fermor, on cats

Cat shovel!

    —Gregory Corso, "Marriage"

Wouldn't it be easier if we just named all the cats Password?

    —Sigrid Nunez, *The Friend*

There was a purity and seriousness to the cat's simple wish to be fucked immediately that Marian found refreshing.

—Nicholson Baker, *The Fermata*

Mkgnao!

—James Joyce, *Ulysses*

Deep feeling doesn't make for good poetry. A way with language would be a bit of help.

—Thom Gunn

Almost all poetry is a failure because it sounds like somebody saying, Look, I have written a poem!

—Charles Bukowski

You could take winos off the sidewalk in front of the drugstore and teach them to be poets in half an hour.

—Nell Zink, *Mislaid*

Open all the mail away from your face.

—Advice for the poetry editor, in Don Paterson's *Best Thought, Worst Thought*

When he is very sick, every man wants his mother.

—Philip Roth, *The Anatomy Lesson*

In the end, every hypochondriac is his own prophet.

—Robert Lowell

When an American sneezes, which should be thrown away, the paper handkerchief or the American?

—Auberon Waugh, *Closing the Circle*

Maybe beauty is medicine quivering on the spoon.

—Lucia Perillo, "Fubar"

Hope is a kind of rigor. Despair is sugar.

—Aravind Adiga, *Amnesty*

Despair busies one, and my weekend was spoken for.

—Joseph O'Neill, *Netherland*

—Do you want to go to bed with *every* woman you meet?
—Yes, I do.

—William Carlos Williams's wife's question, and his answer

The only proof we have of intelligent design is that Adam could not connect his mouth and his penis.

—Amit Majmudar, *Dothead*

A man wouldn't have two-thirds of the problems he has if he didn't venture off to get fucked.

—Philip Roth, *The Dying Animal*

Clock strikes—going out to make love.

—Lord Byron, diary

Shall I compare thee to your place or mine?

> —Veronica Geng, *Love Trouble Is My Business*

He could not fucking die. How could he leave? How could he go?
Everything he hated was here.

> —Philip Roth, *Sabbath's Theater*

No single thing abides; and all things are fucked up.

> —Philip K. Dick, *The Transmigration of Timothy Archer*

Death has this much to be said for it:
You don't have to get out of bed for it.
Wherever you happen to be,
They bring it to you—*free*.

> —Kingsley Amis

The one experience I shall never describe.

> —Virginia Woolf

And then will come the day when the last person who remembers
me will die.

> —Vladimir Nabokov, *The Eye*

Even the living were only ghosts in the making.

> —Pat Barker, *The Ghost Road*

It's rather disconcerting to realize that you can't take even a
book with you.

> —Drue Heinz

Life passes into pages if it passes into anything.

 —James Salter

I feed the pages to the giant blue bullfrog.

 —Kurt Vonnegut, Jr., on corner mailboxes, in *A Man Without a Country*

He was an unshucked oyster, hurtling on the winds, all air, gonad and gut.

 —Barry Hannah, *Bats Out of Hell*

You can squeeze my lemon 'til the juice run down my leg.

 —Robert Johnson, "Traveling Riverside Blues (Take 1)"

The shock of standing again under the wide pale sky, completely exposed. This must be what the oyster feels when the lemon juice falls.

 —Edward St. Aubyn, *Bad News*

No, I do not weep at the world—I am too busy sharpening my oyster knife.

 —Zora Neale Hurston, *How It Feels to Be Colored Me*

Go to where the silence is and say something.

 —Amy Goodman's advice for journalists, in *Columbia Journalism Review*

Write beautifully what people don't want to hear.

 —Frederick Seidel, *Paris Review* interview

I like beautiful melodies telling me terrible things.

    —Tom Waits

If they give you ruled paper, write the other way.

    —Juan Ramón Jiménez

[My mother's] way of teaching me about sex was giving me Colette to read.

    —Patricia Bosworth, *The Men in My Life*

I don't think much of Sade as a writer, although I enjoyed beating off to him as a child.

    —Mary Gaitskill, interview

Even glancing at his throat made me lose my place in Montaigne.

    —Mary Lee Settle, *The Scapegoat*

Howard preferred literate sex. Of course, if that wasn't available, he'd take anything.

    —T. Gertler, *Elbowing the Seducer*

All that short story heat!

    —Lorrie Moore, on an affair between Donald Barthelme and Grace Paley, *See What Can Be Done*

Try to preserve the author's style if he is an author and has a style.

    —Wolcott Gibbs, "Theory and Practice of Editing *New Yorker* Articles"

The worse the writer is, the more argument.

    —Harold Ross, *Letters from the Editor*

If you tapped this sentence at one end, it would never stop rocking.

    —Rogers E. M. Whitaker

This will cut like butter.

    —Wolcott Gibbs

I am distraught at your defection, but since you never actually write anything, I should say I am notionally distraught.

    —Tina Brown, to George W. S. Trow

She wasn't doing a thing that I could see, except standing there leaning on the balcony railing, holding the universe together.

    —J. D. Salinger, "A Girl I Knew"

Youth, beauty, strength: the criteria for physical love are exactly the same as those for Nazism.

    —Michel Houllebecq, *The Possibility of an Island*

If there's one thing you can say for fascism, it had some good poets.

    —Sally Rooney, *Conversations with Friends*

Say what you will about Charles Manson; he really empowered women to pursue excellence in traditionally male-dominated fields.

    —Caitlin Flanagan, in *The Atlantic*

Her eyes shone with Manson girl intent.

    —Rupert Everett, on Madonna, *Red Carpets and Other Banana Skins*

To what extent should the attractive feel responsible for the
sufferings of their admirers?
    —Peter J. Conradi, *Iris Murdoch: A Life*

I'm not even beautiful, but I can lay my hand on beauty.
    —Sheila Heti, *Motherhood*

What is the most beautiful in virile men is something feminine;
what is most beautiful in feminine women is something masculine.
    —Susan Sontag

The real curse of Eve.
    —Jean Rhys, on the thirst to be beautiful and desired, *The Left Bank*

If you're afraid of movies that excite your senses, you're afraid
of movies.
    —Pauline Kael, "Fear of Movies"

Always make the audience suffer as much as possible.
    —Alfred Hitchcock

Our planet's groans at the weight of Hollywood sitting on its face.
    —Rupert Everett, *Red Carpets and Other Banana Skins*

Purviews of cunning abstractions.
    —Robert Coover, *Going Out for a Beer*

New ideas must use old buildings.
    —Jane Jacobs, *The Death and Life of Great American Cities*

The house expressed surprise.

> —Gish Jen, *The Resisters*

Is Your Cornice Necessary?

> —Title of a television series proposed by Kenneth Clark

I did not fully understand the dreaded term "terminal illness" until I saw Heathrow for myself.

> —Dennis Potter, in *The Sunday Times* (London)

I am far from those I am with, and far from those I have left.

> —Edna O'Brien, *The Love Object*

I had been alone more than I could have been had I gone by myself.

> —Sylvia Plath

To be adult is to be alone.

> —Jean Rostand, *The Substance of Man*

We're all so curiously alone. But it's important to keep making signals through the glass.

> —John Updike, in *Life* magazine

We never really see each other, we never say the things we should like to.

> —Marcel Proust, *In Search of Lost Time*

I was risking the possibility of a life where in the "In Case of Emergency Contact" space, I would repeatedly be writing "Me."

> —Lorrie Moore, "One Hot Summer, or a Brief History of Time"

I've fucked up my life. I'm angry because I've fucked up my life.

—Sonia Orwell, in David Plante's *Difficult Women*

You've got ten fingers. Why not stick them in ten pies?

—Michael Frayn, *Against Entropy*

The pie full of white wine . . . being the greatest draught that ever I did see a woman drink in my life.

—Samuel Pepys, diary

It's so beautifully arranged on the plate—you know someone's fingers have been all over it.

—Julia Child, on nouvelle cuisine

Plate after plate after fucking plate.

—Sam Pink, *The Ice Cream Man and Other Stories*

There is always one escape: *into wickedness.* Always do the thing that will shock and wound people.

—George Orwell, "Benefit of Clergy: Some Notes on Salvador Dalí"

All cruel people describe themselves as paragons of frankness!

—Tennessee Williams, *The Milk Train Doesn't Stop Here Anymore*

The sorry indignities that pass as currency between us in lieu of gentler tender.

—Donald Antrim, *The Hundred Brothers*

You always pull out Swift, when you are doing something
disgusting.
—Philip Roth

It isn't that there's no right and wrong here. There's no right.
—V. S. Naipaul, *A Bend in the River*

Assent—and you are sane—
Demur—you're straightaway dangerous—
And handled with a Chain—
—Emily Dickinson

I liked the English, with their hooting, stammering voices, their
toasts, their Stilton and port, their light morals.
—Diane Johnson, *Natural Opium*

Grey little fey little island.
—Cyril Connolly, on England, *The Unquiet Grave*

Think of what our Nation stands for,
Books from Boots' and country lanes,
Free speech, free passes, class distinction,
Democracy and proper drains.
—John Betjeman, "In Westminster Abbey"

If you merchandise tasteless little blobs of dough, you can sell
billions of them by calling them "English" muffins.
—Paul Fussell, *Class*

It is a little known fact that the Queen has a marvelous sense
of humor, especially if one tickles the soles of her feet with an
ostrich feather.

—Auberon Waugh, *The Diaries of Auberon Waugh*

Poets think they're pitchers when they're really catchers.

—Jack Spicer

Is encouragement what the poet needs? . . . Maybe he needs
discouragement.

—Robert Fitzgerald

What I could use at the moment is
a little destruction perpetrated in my favor.

—A. R. Ammons, "Positions"

Rust their typewriters a little, be sea air! be noxious! kill them,
if you must, but stop their poetry!

—Kenneth Koch, "Fresh Air"

If it is broken, so am I.

—Deborah Levy, on her laptop, *Hot Milk*

If we don't post it, it never happened.

—Samantha Hunt, *Mr. Splitfoot*

I will send a picture too
if you will send me one of you.

—Robert Creeley, "The Conspiracy"

Maybe googling people kills them.

—Meg Wolitzer, *The Interestings*

To live is to war with trolls.

—Henrik Ibsen

Somebody put it on the Internet and it went bacterial.

—Donald Hall, *A Carnival of Losses*

Waiting for some lover
to kick me out of bed
for having acted on a whim.

—Paul Muldoon, "Maggot"

If somebody liked to dress up in chamois leather and be stung by
wasps, I really couldn't see why one should stop him.

—Kenneth Tynan, quoting Robert Morley, *The Diaries of Kenneth Tynan*

A polymorphous game of button-button with sweetmeats at the end.

—Robert Christgau, describing a make-out session, *Going into the City*

How can he be killed most easily? With the fewest stains?

—Donald Barthelme, *Snow White*

I have joined an ancient fraternity. I have killed a man.

—Hubert Selby, Jr., *Waiting Period*

You're Nobody 'Til Somebody Kills You.

—The Notorious B.I.G., song title

For me violent moments are always existential moments. They are crucial.

— Norman Mailer, *Paris Review* interview

What then, art director? Graphics consultant? What is the layout? It is this: to shoot him from behind, somewhere on the top of the gorge.

— James Dickey, *Deliverance*

That corpse you planted last year in your garden,
Has it begun to sprout?

— T. S. Eliot, *The Waste Land*

I may have never killed any one, but I have read some obituary notices with great satisfaction.

— Clarence Darrow, *The Story of My Life*

Dear God, please make me stop writing like a woman.

— Dorothy Parker

It is difficult for a woman to define her feelings in language which is chiefly made by men to express theirs.

— Thomas Hardy, *Far from the Madding Crowd*

Shyness is shit. It isn't cute or feminine or appealing. It's torment, and it's shit.

— Octavia E. Butler, *Bloodchild and Other Stories*

Heaven preserve me from littleness and pleasantness and smoothness.

— Violet Trefusis, letter to Vita Sackville-West

The Anglo-Saxon idea that you can be rude with impunity to any female who has written a book is utterly *damnable*.

> —Jean Rhys, letter

"Women's fiction" doesn't sound like anything but a slur to my ears.

> —Sheila Heti

Feminism hasn't failed, it's just never been tried.

> —Hilary Mantel

Were all women devastatingly superior to men, or was it just these two compared to me?

> —Gish Jen, *The Resisters*

If I'm going to skate, I'm going to race.

> —Ken Kesey, interview

We ice-skated to "Eve of Destruction."

> —Lorrie Moore, *Who Will Run the Frog Hospital?*

Every writer is a skater, and must go partly where he would, and partly where the skates carry him.

> —Ralph Waldo Emerson

Until you've potato-raced against a congenital one-legged man in a sack you haven't potato-raced.

> —Stanley Elkin, *The Dick Gibson Show*

Snobbery is a form of despair.

> —Joseph Brodsky, interview

I expect I am something of a snob . . . I am pleased to be friends with people of distinguished lineage.
    —Isaiah Berlin, *Affirming*

Virginians are all snobs, and I like snobs. A snob has to spend so much time being a snob that he has little left to meddle with you.
    —William Faulkner

Elitism is reprehensible only when it is snobbish and exclusive. The best sort of elitism tries to expand the elite by encouraging more and more people to join it.
    —Richard Dawkins, *Brief Candle in the Dark*

All women under the sun are unscrupulous if there is something they want.
    —Muriel Spark, *The Bachelors*

When boys get angry with each other, they just fight it out and it's all over. But girls are dirty. They pretend to be your friend and go behind your back.
    —Mary Gaitskill, *Bad Behavior*

Women dress alike all over the world: they dress to be annoying to other women.
    —Elsa Schiaparelli

She wears her Cloaths as if they were thrown on with a Pitch-Fork.
    —Jonathan Swift

Her only flair is in her nostrils.

—Pauline Kael

The sun shone, having no alternative, on the nothing new.

—Opening line of Samuel Beckett's *Murphy*

I have suffered the atrocity of sunsets.

—Sylvia Plath, "Elm"

The sun is a joke.

—Nathanael West, *The Day of the Locust*

Some Englishman once said that marriage is a long dull meal with the pudding served first.

—Julian Barnes, *The Sense of an Ending*

Take this pudding away. It has no theme.

—Winston Churchill

To call it pudding and so relate it to rice and tapioca would be an insult.

—Virginia Woolf, *A Room of One's Own*

Make a remark, said the Red Queen, it's ridiculous to leave all the conversation to the pudding.

—Lewis Carroll, *Through the Looking-Glass*

Forty—sombre anniversary to the hedonist.

—Cyril Connolly, *The Unquiet Grave*

Beware of using up your last forty years in being the curator of your first fifty.

    —Allan Gurganus, *Oldest Living Confederate Widow Tells All*

At seventy, I'm at last more at ease with what Homer Simpson called his womanly needs.

    —Les Murray, *Killing the Black Dog*

One cannot think well, love well, sleep well, if one has not dined well.

    —Virginia Woolf, *A Room of One's Own*

Of course reading and thinking are important but, my God, food is important too.

    —Iris Murdoch, *The Sea, the Sea*

Ham held the same rating as the basic black dress. If you had a ham in the meat house any situation could be faced.

    —Edna Lewis, *The Taste of Country Cooking*

Love isn't saying, I love you, but calling to say, did you eat?

    —Marlon James, *The Book of Night Women*

What has love ever meant to me but creaking stairs in other people's houses?

    —Iris Murdoch, *Under the Net*

I want to hear raucous music, to see faces, to brush against bodies, to drink fiery Benedictine.

    —Anaïs Nin, diary

Anything that gets your blood racing is probably worth doing.

—Hunter S. Thompson, attributed

A ship is safe in harbor, but that's not what ships are for.

—William G. T. Shedd, attributed

Let other people frequent nightclubs in their tight-ass skirts and Live. I'm just sitting here, vibrating in my apartment, at having been given this one chance to live.

—Sheila Heti, *How Should a Person Be?*

Cherish your old apartments and pause for a moment when you pass them. Pay tribute, for they are the caretakers for your reinventions.

—Colson Whitehead, *The Colossus of New York*

The West Side Writing and Asthma Club.

—Club cofounded by Groucho Marx

She was just as pretty as a peeled onion.

—Nate Shaw, on a mule, in *All God's Dangers*

A mule will labor ten years willingly and patiently for you, for the privilege of kicking you once.

—William Faulkner

A small-bore man, over his head, and riding a bad horse.

—Ben Bradlee, on Ron Ziegler, Nixon's press secretary, *A Good Life*

Nothing is more terrible than ignorance with spurs on.

—Johann Wolfgang von Goethe

Very ugly emotions perhaps make a poem.

—Robert Lowell, *Paris Review* interview

He put his woes in verse,
And sold them to a magazine.

—Paul Laurence Dunbar, "Then and Now"

What
ought a poem to be? Answer, *a sad*
and angry consolation.

—Geoffrey Hill, *The Triumph of Love*

You aint gonna believe this . . . Somebody has been fuckin my
watermelons . . . damn near screwed the whole patch.

—Cormac McCarthy, *Suttree*

Red cold
guffaw of summer,
slice
of watermelon!

—José Juan Tablada, "Haiku" (translated by Samuel Beckett)

Let us always have a vast condom within us to protect the health of
our soul amid the filth into which it is plunged.

—Gustave Flaubert, *The Letters of Gustave Flaubert: 1830–1857*

The only thing you can depend on with condoms is that they will take 20 to 50 percent off your fuck.

—Norman Mailer, in conversation with Madonna

Smiles, bells, parades, horses, bleh. If so, please add an orgy. If an orgy would help, don't hesitate.

—Ursula K. Le Guin, *The Ones Who Walk Away from Omelas*

We stage an orgie—so delightful that it knocks me out.

—Theodore Dreiser, *The American Diaries, 1902–1926*

An austere orgy is no orgy at all.

—John D. MacDonald, *Dress Her in Indigo*

I believe in getting into hot water. I think it keeps you clean.

—G. K. Chesterton

There must be quite a few things a hot bath won't cure, but I don't know many of them.

—Sylvia Plath, *The Bell Jar*

The hot tub—a sous vide bath of genitalia.

—Anna Wiener, *Uncanny Valley*

I think I'll take a bath so I can have a faucet orgasm.

—Jay McInerney, *Story of My Life*

Everything is miraculous. It is miraculous that one does not melt in one's bath.

—Pablo Picasso

Existentialism means that no one else can take a bath for you.

—Delmore Schwartz, "Existentialism: The Inside Story"

I have had a good many more uplifting thoughts, creative and expansive visions—while soaking in comfortable baths or drying myself after bracing showers—in well-equipped American bathrooms than I have ever had in any cathedral.

—Edmund Wilson, *A Piece of My Mind*

You can tell a lot from a person's nails. When a life starts to unravel, they're among the first to go.

—Ian McEwan, *Saturday*

[Anna Wintour] wanted to work for *Interview*, but . . . I don't think she knows how to dress, she's actually a terrible dresser.

—Andy Warhol, *The Andy Warhol Diaries*

Nuclear Wintour.

—Tabloid nickname

If Botticelli were alive today he'd be working for *Vogue*.

—Peter Ustinov, in *The Observer*

Don't read women's magazines. They're bad for your stomach.

—Kate Tempest, "These Things I Know"

The magazines pile up and die.

—Karl Shapiro, *The Bourgeois Poet*

The greatest pleasure I know, is to do a good action by stealth, and to have it found out by accident.

—Charles Lamb

Love with your mouth shut, help without breaking your ass or publicizing it: keep cool, but care.

—Thomas Pynchon, V

God damn it, you've got to be kind.

—Kurt Vonnegut, Jr., *God Bless You, Mr. Rosewater*

My sad conviction is that people can only agree about what they're not really interested in.

—Bertrand Russell

Acceptance is usually more a matter of fatigue than anything else.

—David Foster Wallace

When people call you intelligent it is almost always because they agree with you. Otherwise they call you arrogant.

—Nassim Nicholas Taleb

You must decide to drink wine *in quantity*.

—Kingsley Amis, *On Drink*

Isn't it amazing . . . how a full bottle of wine isn't enough for two people any more?

—John Updike, "Gesturing"

Like some wines our love could neither mature nor travel.

—Graham Greene, *The Comedians*

Let's shuck an obligation.

—John Berryman, "Dream Song 82: Op. posth. no. 5"

Several excuses are always less convincing than one.

—Aldous Huxley, *Point Counter Point*

We are not saints, but we have kept our appointment. How many people can boast as much?

—Samuel Beckett, *Waiting for Godot*

Punctuality is the virtue of the bored.

—Evelyn Waugh

The chronically unpunctual should cancel all engagements for a definite period.

—Cyril Connolly, *The Unquiet Grave*

Miss Otis regrets she's unable to lunch today.

—Cole Porter, "Miss Otis Regrets"

I don't mind telling people awful things if I can make them funny.

—Lucia Berlin, "Silence"

It's hard to be told to *lighten up* because if you lighten up any more, you're going to float the fuck away.

—Roxane Gay, *Bad Feminist*

Most people are clever because they don't know how to be honest.

—William Gaddis, *The Recognitions*

And so we "bluff" . . . We all do it. Let us despise ourselves for doing it, but not one another.

—Max Beerbohm, *The Prince of Minor Writers*

I wonder whether all my ironies aren't simply one more way of sucking up to the ruling class.

—Mary-Kay Wilmers, *Human Relations and Other Difficulties*

Irony is just honesty with the volume cranked up.

—George Saunders

It's the hardest addiction of all . . . Forget heroin. Just try giving up irony.

—Edward St. Aubyn, *At Last*

The idea of Herman Melville in a writing class is always distressing to me.

—Harold Bloom, *Paris Review* interview

Everywhere I go I'm asked if I think universities stifle writers. I think they don't stifle enough of them.

—Flannery O'Connor, interview

Call me a science fiction writer. I'll come to your house and I'll nail your pet's head to a coffee table.

—Harlan Ellison, according to his *New York Times* obituary

I wouldn't leave him with enough teeth to pronounce "smutty."

> —John D. MacDonald, on the man who called him a smutty
> book writer

It's always the worst people who happen to burst in on you when you are in misery.

> —Muriel Spark, *A Good Comb*

The grand never-knocker.

> —Chang-rae Lee, *Native Speaker*

Damn we were lonely people, the two of us.

> —Jonathan Miles, *Dear American Airlines*

Solitude is an Anglo-Saxon concept. In Mexico City, if you're the only person on a bus and someone gets on they'll not only come next to you, they will lean against you.

> —Lucia Berlin, "Fool to Cry"

I remember loneliness crushing first my lungs, then my heart, then my balls.

> —Denis Johnson, *Jesus' Son*

My chest bumps like a dryer with shoes in it.

> —David Foster Wallace, *Infinite Jest*

When you're alone like he was alone . . .

> —T. S. Eliot, *Sweeney Agonistes*

The frying pan's too wide.

> —Joni Mitchell, on loneliness, "My Old Man"

Nuts to the educational value of suffering.

> —Robert Christgau, *Going into the City*

How did you become a four-line seventy-five-cents-a-word
advertisement in the back pages of *The New York Review of Books*?

> —Donald Barthelme, *The Teachings of Don B.*

Abandonitis.

> —Roland Barthes, *Mourning Diary*

How good the water felt when you got your bath
from one of those
big tubs that folk in chicago barbecue in.

> —Nikki Giovanni, "Nikki-Rosa"

When the Caliph Omar destroyed the libraries of Alexandria he
is supposed to have kept the public baths warm for eighteen days
with burning manuscripts.

> —George Orwell, *As I Please, 1943–1946*

The book-bed-bath defense system.

> —Cyril Connolly, on warding off depression, *The Unquiet Grave*

That's just common sense: if you're going to buy a pair of pants
you want them to be tight enough so everyone will want to go to
bed with you.

> —Frank O'Hara, "Personism: A Manifesto"

—Girls now, they wear leggings. As pants. It's embarrassing.

—Just parading their coochies around town.

>—Stephanie Danler, *Sweetbitter*

Melodrama crouches upon the brim of his sombrero.

>—Max Beerbohm, *The Works of Max Beerbohm*

Oh my god! Shakespeare. That multiform & encyclopedic bastard.

>—John Berryman

There is one fascinating view which maintains that all the mystery is utterly clarified if we suppose that everyone is roaring drunk.

>—Delmore Schwartz, on *Hamlet*, in *The Ego Is Always at the Wheel: Bagatelles*

The way to see the world was to see it drunk. Everything was created to be seen drunk.

>—Patricia Highsmith, *Strangers on a Train*

Did you often stagger into the middle of busy intersections with your gummy eyes and make comical, drunken attempts to direct traffic?

>—Charles Portis, *The Masters of Atlantis*

The gibbous moon hung over the planet Earth, a dead thing over a dying thing.

>—John Fowles, *The Magus*

Nobody wanted to hear that America's ascent to the moon had been made with a ladder of bones.

—Michael Chabon, *Moonglow*

If Gus Grissom had had a heart attack on the moon, nobody in the whole world would be able to look up into the sky with the same awe and wonder as before.

—Joy Williams, "Summer"

He was like the bed at a party on which they pile the coats.

—George Saunders, *Tenth of December*

They treated me like an open manhole.

—Ring Lardner, "Ex Parte"

I am the self-consumer of my woes.

—John Clare, "I Am!"

A man who gives a good account of himself is probably lying, since any life when viewed from the inside is simply a series of defeats.

—George Orwell, *As I Please, 1943–1946*

Sometimes I think nothing is simple but the feeling of pain.

—Lester Bangs, *Psychotic Reactions and Carburetor Dung*

If you didn't write, I'd only get mail from the IRS.

—Breece D'J Pancake, in *A Room Forever*

I really wish that I were dead.

—Frederick Nietzsche, "Song of a Theocritean Goatherd"

—How many staffers does it take to change a light bulb at Time,
  Inc.?

—Twenty-five. One to screw in the bulb, and twenty-four to stand
  around talking about how great the old bulb used to be.

> —Terry McDonell, *The Accidental Life*

Only the Brits can think the right level of malignant thoughts a
magazine requires.

> —Robert Hughes, in Tina Brown's *The Vanity Fair Diaries*

Never lose your sense of the superficial.

> —Lord Northcliffe's advice for tabloid journalists

It was a gimmick—everything is, and if it isn't, that's its gimmick.

> —Joshua Cohen, *Book of Numbers*

Lists are a form of cultural hysteria.

> —Don DeLillo, *Paris Review* interview

Lists are a form of power.

> —A. S. Byatt, *The Virgin in the Garden*

Christ! What are patterns for?

> —Amy Lowell, "Patterns"

Every man who swaggers is fraudulent.

> —Norman Mailer

All the little gods of irony must whoop and weep and roll on the floors of Olympus when they tune in on the night thoughts of a truly fatuous male.

—John D. MacDonald, *The Deep Blue Good-By*

My knuckles? Well dragged.

—Colson Whitehead, *Sag Harbor*

Who wants to read about another nifty guy at loose ends?

—Jim Harrison, *Paris Review* interview

I reflected wearily that it was not easy to be a Woman in these stirring times. I said it then and I say it now: it just isn't our century.

—Elaine Dundy, *The Dud Avocado*

This holy radionovela brought to you by Female Sadness Incorporated.

—Juliana Delgado Lopera, *Fiebre Tropical*

Everything but the bloodhounds snappin' at her rear end.

—Thelma Ritter, in *All About Eve*

You may not be interested in absurdity, she said firmly, but absurdity is interested in *you*.

—Donald Barthelme, "A Shower of Gold"

I think I am going to be an adventuress, I said. Is it all right?

—Eve Babitz, *Eve's Hollywood*

Printed by the weird sisters in the year of the big wind.

—James Joyce, *Ulysses*

Everything's weird if you look long enough.

—Sam Lipsyte, "The Dungeon Master"

The rewards for being sane may not be very many, but knowing what's funny is one of them.

—Kingsley Amis, *Stanley and the Women*

For what do we live, but to make sport for our neighbors, and laugh at them in our turn?

—Jane Austen, *Pride and Prejudice*

I am not the fig plucker but the fig plucker's son, and I can pluck figs until the fig plucker comes.

—Collegiate graffiti

Naturally there is no known rejoinder to this.

—William Faulkner, *Absalom, Absalom*

It is almost a joke, but a joke that nobody tells.

—Hilary Mantel, *Wolf Hall*

There's no such thing as a joke.

—Joe Orton

Nothing's a joke with me. It just all comes out like one.

—Lorrie Moore, *The Collected Stories*

Does my carbon footprint look big in this?

    —Laura Freeman, in *The Spectator*

Madame, this is a restaurant, not a meadow.

    —Waiter to Greta Garbo, in *Ninotchka*, after she orders raw carrots
      and beets for lunch

I can't bear to go to another restaurant and see the sneeze guard over
the salad bar.

    —Joy Williams, "Shepherd"

The best choice is always the restaurant fifteen minutes further than
you are willing to go.

    —Jonathan Gold

If you would ask the waiter to bring a fairly sharp knife, I could cut
off a nice little block of the atmosphere, to take home with me.

    —Dorothy Parker, "Just a Little One"

That cult of the belly, I say, breeds wind.

    —Gustave Flaubert

What if we just went home and read books to each other?

    —Gary Shteyngart, *Super Sad True Love Story*

People with no upper-body strength, who read poetry. These are
my people.

    —Caitlin Moran, *How to Build a Girl*

No restaurants. The means of consoling oneself: reading cookbooks.

    —Baudelaire

Decayed literature makes the richest of all soils.

— Henry David Thoreau, journal

In the modern world the stupid are cocksure while the intelligent are full of doubt.

— Bertrand Russell, "The Triumph of Stupidity"

Every man has a right to be stupid, but comrade Macdonald abuses the privilege.

— Leon Trotsky, on Dwight Macdonald

Braininess is not attractive unless combined with some signs of elegance; *class*.

— Alice Munro, "The Beggar Maid"

Just because people love your mind,
Doesn't mean they have to love your body, too.

— Richard Brautigan, *Rommel Drives on Deep in Egypt*

Stephanie, I want to ask you something, all right? Do you think that I am either interesting or intelligent?

— John Travolta, in *Saturday Night Fever*

Except for socially, you're my role model.

— Joan Cusack, to Holly Hunter, in *Broadcast News*

When you're really cute that's all you have to be, you make a career out of it. Someone asks you what you do, you say, "Nothing. I'm cute."

— Elmore Leonard, *Killshot*

Whatever you do, ya' gotta be sexy.

—Dr. John

Maybe I have Attention Surplus Disorder.

—Susan Sontag, *Paris Review* interview

People always know more than I do, but what I know I know.

—Richard Ford, in *The Guardian*

My 60-watt lighted head.

—Sylvia Plath, *Journals*

I drank coffee and read old books and waited for the year to end.

—Richard Brautigan, *Trout Fishing in America*

Peoples bore me,
literature bores me, especially great literature.

—John Berryman, "Dream Song #14"

There is nothing like a good book to put you to sleep with the illusion that life is rich and meaningful.

—Robert Penn Warren, *All the King's Men*

I don't want to sound like a misanthrope, but there's something wrong with us.

—Ishmael Reed, *Paris Review* interview

She felt that she was feeding something inside her that belonged in a pen in the zoo.

—Joy Williams, "Winter Chemistry"

Do as I do. *Break with the outside world*, live like a bear.

— Gustave Flaubert, *The Letters of Gustave Flaubert: 1830–1857*

Boxing makes you want to eat, but eating does not make you want to box.

— A. J. Liebling, *Between Meals*

I want to keep fighting because it is the only thing that keeps me out of the hamburger joints. If I don't fight, I'll eat this planet.

— George Foreman

I hate life. There: I have said it; I'll not take it back.

— Gustave Flaubert, *The Letters of Gustave Flaubert: 1830–1857*

If you expect nothing from somebody you are never disappointed.

— Sylvia Plath, *The Bell Jar*

Pessimism does win us great happy moments.

— Max Beerbohm, *The Prince of Minor Writers*

I was afraid I was goin to die and then I was afraid I wasnt.

— Cormac McCarthy, *Blood Meridian*

My anger subsides, I'd like to pee.

— Samuel Beckett, *Endgame*

There's no use in denying it: this has been a bad week. I've started drinking my own urine.

— Bret Easton Ellis, *American Psycho*

Once you had pissed in the sink of your bathless double you
belonged to the fallen world around you.

—Robert Stone

Male urination is a form of commentary.

—Camille Paglia, *Sexual Personae*

The other day a dog peed on me. A bad sign.

—H. L. Mencken, letter to Theodore Dreiser

Catch your first morning urine in your hands
and splash it on that rash.

—Poison ivy cure in Elizabeth Alexander's poem "talk radio, d.c."

I'm ready to fall in love with life.
I'm ready to drink her pee.
I'll take a shower after.

—Frederick Seidel, "Too Much"

I think about you when I go to the bathroom.

—Martha Plimpton, to River Phoenix, in *The Mosquito Coast*

I think about you so much, I forget to use the bathroom.

—Seymour Cassel, to Gena Rowlands, in *Minnie and Moskowitz*

And, of course men know best about everything, except what
women know better.

—George Eliot, *Middlemarch*

I find that those men who are personally most polite to women, who call them angels and all that, cherish in secret the greatest contempt for them.

    —Germaine Greer, *The Female Eunuch*

To speak up is not about speaking louder, it is about feeling entitled to voice a wish.

    —Deborah Levy, *Things I Don't Want to Know*

No need to hurry. No need to sparkle. No need to be anybody but oneself.

    —Virginia Woolf, *A Room of One's Own*

Pray always for all the learned, the oblique, the delicate. Let them not be quite forgotten at the throne of God when the simple come into their kingdom.

    —Evelyn Waugh

Cultural allusions?—forget it. You can't assume the audience knows *anything* beyond the latest thong-snappings in the supermarket tabloids.

    —James Wolcott, *Critical Mass*

That's all we have, finally, the words, and they had better be the right ones.

    —Raymond Carver, *Call If You Need Me*

Windbags can be right. Aphorists can be wrong. It is a tough world.

    —James Fenton, in *The Times* (London)

The itch of a lost quotation in a book you cannot find.

> —Hannah Sullivan, "The Sandpit After Rain"

Of course you don't like all the aphorisms. I don't like all of you.

> —Don Paterson, *Best Thought, Worst Thought*

I believe in the fatal hairdo just for the love of saying *fatal hairdo*.

> —Lucia Perillo, "Urban Legend"

That upsweeping electric hair is the poet's helmet, his rooster comb.

> —Alfred Kazin, *Alfred Kazin's Journals*

Gimme an upsweep, Minnie,
With humpteen baby curls.

> —Gwendolyn Brooks, "at the hairdresser's"

Smile like a hairdresser
Giving Cameron Diaz a shampoo.

> —Charles Simic, "O Spring"

—What do you call Khrushchev's hairdo?
—Harvest of 1963.

> —Joke in Francis Spufford's *Red Plenty*

Darling, I was going to ask you, what happened to it? You could have fought back. Or did they give you an anesthetic?

> —Malcolm Bradbury, on a haircut, *Eating People Is Wrong*

It is impossible to be angry for very long with a man who wears a wig.

> —Auberon Waugh, *Diaries of Auberon Waugh*

I'd go and get my hair cut, I was so lonely for some fingers.
—Peter Orner, *Maggie Brown and Others*

The America I loved still exists at the front desks of our public libraries.
—Kurt Vonnegut, Jr., *A Man Without a Country*

Virtually every second book in every library in the world is irreparably deteriorating because of brittle paper and acid content.
—David Markson, *Reader's Block*

After three days without reading, talk becomes flavorless.
—Chinese proverb

Nothing beats sitting around in the daytime with a novel on your lap and—truthfully—telling yourself you're working.
—Kingsley Amis, "Report on a Fiction Prize"

The slight sense of degeneracy induced by reading novels before luncheon.
—Elizabeth Bowen, *The Hotel*

Novels are crazy!
—Robert Menasse, *The Capital*

When we read a novel, we are insane—bonkers.
—Ursula K. Le Guin

I wish one could press
snowflakes in a book like flowers.
—James Schuyler, "February 13, 1975"

Make yourself at home, Frank—hit somebody.

—Don Rickles, to Frank Sinatra, on *The Tonight Show*

It is perfectly all right to cast the first stone,
if you have some more in your pocket.

—Bob Kaufman, "Heavy Water Blues"

Violence is the repartee of the illiterate.

—Alan Brien, in *Punch*

Come closer, boys. It will be easier for you.

—Erskine Childers, while facing a firing squad

What a remarkable anthology one could make of pieces of writing
describing executions!

—George Orwell, *As I Please, 1943–1946*

If you cannot speak truth at a beheading, when can you speak it?

—Hilary Mantel, *The Mirror & the Light*

Here is the Strangler, reading the *Kenyon Review*! Good luck to you,
Strangler!

—Kenneth Koch, "Fresh Air"

The bad luck of other people reaffirmed that I was doing okay.

—Rachel Kushner, *The Mars Room*

Sometimes luck is a splash of mud from an oncoming bus.

—Elizabeth Jane Howard, *Mr. Wrong*

The reams
of shit I've read.

> —James Schuyler, "Dining Out with Doug and Frank"

It is better to be quotable than to be honest.

> —Tom Stoppard

Honesty, for me, is usually the worst policy imaginable.

> —Patricia Highsmith

Once love had seemed like magic. Now it seemed like tricks.

> —Lorrie Moore, *Like Life*

We've gotten along. We've never felt like congratulating ourselves.

> —Denis Johnson, on a long marriage, *The Largesse of the Sea Maiden*

One doesn't have to get anywhere in a marriage. It's not a public
conveyance.

> —Iris Murdoch, *A Severed Head*

One can't explain one's marriage.

> —Henry James, *The Portrait of a Lady*

Against all odds, honey, we're the big door prize.

> —John Prine, "In Spite of Ourselves" (duet with Iris Dement)

I am not fit to marry. I am often cross, and I like my own way,
and I have a distaste for men.

> —Anthony Trollope, *He Knew He Was Right*

The night he and Kate married, Kate's cousin Freeman had wired a cowbell to their bedsprings.

—Prank described in Donald Hall's *A Carnival of Losses*

Blush like you mean it.

—Erica Jong, *Fear of Flying*

The blush: what evolutionary advantage do we gain in the *publication* of our embarrassment?

—Don Paterson, *Best Thought, Worst Thought*

The squandermania of the thing.

—James Joyce, *Ulysses*

The airport bookstores did not sell books, only bestsellers, which Sita Dulip cannot read without risking a severe systemic reaction.

—Ursula K. Le Guin, *Changing Planes*

The tin bird whoofed down the runway and lifted sharply, while everybody played the habitual game of total indifference which hides the shallow breathing and contracted sphincters of the Air Age.

—John D. MacDonald, *Dress Her in Indigo*

I do not get on airplanes unless I'm profoundly drunk.

—Harry Crews, letter

We're in the clouds, people! This can't last!

—Sarah Hepola, *Blackout*

Turn your air vents to full, people!

> —Nicholson Baker, on how to keep a crashing plane aloft, *Room Temperature*

Icelandic Air was known by everyone to offer the best bargains in the skies, if glimpses of the red-hot engine parts didn't put you off.

> —David Hare, *The Blue Touch Paper*

Tell yourself you had nothing to live for anyway, so that when the plane crashed it was no big deal.

> —Lorrie Moore, *Like Life*

I'm always very happy when I'm traveling to know that the pilots are better pilots than I am a writer.

> —Gabriel García Márquez

You can't do anything about the length of your life, but you can do something about its width and depth.

> —H. L. Mencken, attributed

The less you eat, drink and read books; the less you go to the theatre, the dance hall, the public-house; the less you think, love, theorize, sing, paint, fence, etc.; the more you *save*—the *greater* becomes your treasure which neither moths nor dust will devour—your *capital*. The less you *are*, the more you *have*; the less you express your own life, the greater is your alienated life—the greater is the store of your estranged being.

> —Karl Marx, *Human Requirements and Division of Labor*

You're you. And that's as important as you want to make it.
> —Samuel R. Delany

I wish I was Bill Murray. I hope everything I've read about evolution is wrong, and I eventually evolve into him.
> —Caitlin Moran, *How to Be a Woman*

We have art in order to not die of the truth.
> —Frederick Nietzsche

Life is a shitstorm, in which art is our only umbrella.
> —Mario Vargas Llosa

Your shit is in the pan, about to get deep-fried.
> —Erika Ellis, *good fences*

When you're in the shit up to your neck, there's nothing left to do but sing.
> —Samuel Beckett

Messy, isn't it?
> —Richard Brautigan, *Sombrero Fallout*

Bills are easier to pay when short ribs are braising in the oven.
> —Michael Ruhlman, *Ruhlman's How to Braise*

Like ribs you are better
the day after, when all
is forgiven.
> —Kevin Young, "Ode to Greens"

Nobody wants to be here and nobody wants to leave.

—Cormac McCarthy, *The Road*

One way of measuring a life—maybe as good a method as any other—is on the basis of how much peculiarity you have helped to generate.

—Ernest Gaines, in Terry McDonell's *The Accidental Life*

Let me say it plainly: our true projects have finally been ourselves.

—Seymour Krim, *What's This Cat's Story?*

Life itself is the proper binge.

—Julia Child, in *Time* magazine

Life's tallest order is to keep the feelings up, to make two dollars' worth of euphoria go the distance.

—Stanley Elkin

With a hey, and a ho, and a hey-nonny-no.

—William Shakespeare, *As You Like It*

And a hot-cha-cha.

—P. G. Wodehouse, *Bertie Wooster Sees Through It*

Down, everybody! Down on all fours! We're going to show you our new step!

—Samuel R. Delany, *Nova*

I don't get much sun lately, Dwight said.

—Denis Johnson, *Angels*

Dwight was tired.

> —Joy Williams, "Rot"

Dwight thinks with his typewriter.

> —Paul Goodman, on Dwight Macdonald

At least Dwight manned up for a few seconds.

> —Bernardine Evaristo, *Girl, Woman, Other*

The ending should fall off the tree like a ripe pear.

> —Andrew Lytle, letter to Harry Crews

Was that it?
Was *that* it?
Was that *it*?
That was it.

> —Howard Nemerov, "A Life"

It was getting late and we each had to find our people.

> —Ta-Nehisi Coates, *The Water Dancer*

We're all just walking each other home.

> —Baba Ram Dass

Thanks for coming. Thanks for showing up, too.

> —Bette Midler, attributed

ACKNOWLEDGMENTS

Thanks to John Stinson, rare book dealer and cheerful misanthrope, for a thousand lessons in the literature of absurdity, parody, dissent, and disturbance. Thanks to Jonathan Miles, John Williams, Sam Tanenhaus, Max Watman, Charles Taylor, David Orr, Julie Truax, and Charles Truax, who commented on early drafts of this manuscript. Thanks to Daniel Okrent for several choice lines from his own commonplace book. Thanks to Penn Garner LeFavour and Harriet Garner LeFavour, my kids, who pitched in mightily during a fact-checking crunch on this book. (Any remaining errors are my own.) Thanks to the New York Public Library and Joe N' Throw coffee shop in Fairmont, West Virginia, where a great deal of this material was stitched together. Thanks to David McCormick, my debonair agent. Thanks to Stig Abell and Rozalind Dineen of the *Times Literary Supplement* (*TLS*), which published an early selection of this material. Thanks also to James Bennet and Brian Zittel of the Sunday Review section of *The New York Times*, which printed another selection of this material. Thanks to Jonathan Galassi at Farrar, Straus and Giroux, who understood this project from the moment I mentioned it to him. Thanks to Rodrigo Corral for his bold and elegant cover design. Thanks also, at FSG, to Jeff Seroy, Chloe Texier-Rose, Brianna Panzica, Richard Oriolo, and Katharine Liptak.

Thanks finally to Cree LeFavour, for everything.

INDEX

PERMISSIONS ACKNOWLEDGMENTS

Grateful acknowledgment is made for permission to reprint the following material:

Lines from "Haiku" by José Juan Tablada, in *Anthology of Mexican Poetry* by Octavio Paz, translated by Samuel Beckett. Copyright © 1965 by Indiana University Press. Reprinted with permission of Indiana University Press.

Lines from "Nikki-Rosa" by Nikki Giovanni, in *The Collected Poetry of Nikki Giovanni*. Compilation copyright © 2003 by Nikki Giovanni. Used by permission of HarperCollins Publishers.

Lines from "No-Fly Zone" by Tracy K. Smith, from *Life on Mars*. Copyright © 2011 by Tracy K. Smith. Reprinted with the permission of The Permis-